Teaching
Mathematics 3–5

Teaching Mathematics 3–5

Developing Learning in the Foundation Stage

Sue Gifford

Open University Press

Open University Press
McGraw-Hill Education
McGraw-Hill House
Shoppenhangers Road
Maidenhead
Berkshire
England
SL6 2QL

email: enquiries@openup.co.uk
world wide web: www.openup.co.uk

and Two Penn Plaza, New York, NY 10121-2289, USA

First published 2005
Reprinted 2008, 2009 (twice)

A catalogue record of this book is available from the British Library

ISBN-10: 0 335 21686 2 (pb)   0 335 21687 0 (hb)
ISBN-13: 978 0335 21686 4 (pb)   978 0335 21687 1 (hb)

Library of Congress Cataloguing-in-Publication Data
CIP data applied for

Typeset by RefineCatch Limited, Bungay, Suffolk
Printed in the UK by Bell & Bain Ltd, Glasgow

Contents

Acknowledgements

I am grateful to the children and staff of many early years settings, including past members of the Number in Early Childhood Group and the Early Childhood Mathematics Group:

Alfred Mizzen First School
All Saints, Carshalton
The Alton Early Years Unit
Balham Nursery School
Beecholme First School
Benedict First School
Burlington Infants School
Cheam Park Farm Infants School
Eastwood Nursery School
Falconbrook Early Years Unit
The Glebe Nursery School
Greenfields Nursery School
Grove House Nursery School
Heathfield Nursery School
Hillbrook Early Years Unit
Maple Infants School
Redford Nursery School
Rowdown Primary School
Somerset Nursery School
Surbiton Hill Nursery School
Triangle Nursery School
The Vanessa Nursery School

and in particular:

Julie Alderton
Peter Afford
Ann Bridges
Mary Coen

Pat Gura
Pauline Wilson

Blockplay illustrations courtesy of:

Froebel Early Childhood Blockplay Project, directed by Tina Bruce, research assistant Pat Gura in collaboration with the Froebel Blockplay Research Group

Introduction
Between the secret garden and the hothouse: recent changes in early years mathematics

I used to spend large amounts of time and effort creating shops with five year olds so that they could learn mathematics through play. We used to arrange and price the goods, I would model the shopkeeper's role and they would pay the correct price with coins. Then I would go off and leave them to it, but inevitably whenever I looked, they were stuffing bags full of goods without paying (i.e. shoplifting) or paying arbitrary amounts and then demanding huge quantities of change from the shopkeeper. Their discussions would not be about the prices but about who was the mummy and who was the baby and what they were going to have for tea. When I went in and asked the price of things, all this seemed to do was to kill the role-play stone dead. As the children were creatively developing their language and social skills, I resolved not to interfere but to focus their mathematical learning elsewhere. So we played shopping games with coins, where the children readily focused on the prices. However, I always felt this as a personal failure: I knew children were supposed to learn mathematics through play.

Some years later, I saw a training video showing a nursery child as shopkeeper, who kept shutting the shop and saying with relish to her customers, 'Its closed!' The commentary said there was a lot of mathematics going on, but it seemed to me that the child was really exploring the power of the shopkeeper's role. On another occasion, a reception teacher and I set out to observe mathematical learning in home-corner play: there were lots of opportunities in laying the table, matching different sized dolls with beds and clothes, and arranging things in cupboards. We watched as some boys donned batman cloaks, grabbed knives from the cutlery drawer, climbed up on the kitchen table, leapt off and seemed about to disembowel the dolls, at which point the teacher stopped them. We decided that there may have been spatial estimation in jumping off the table, but really this was play exploring power and gender roles. I began to conclude that children's role-play was concerned with the larger themes of life, like love and power, rather than mundane things like the price of potatoes.

Research has since confirmed these doubts. Rogers (1996), researching in three countries, found that young children playing in 'fast food' scenarios used literacy skills but did not use any numbers in their play. They tended to concentrate on what they wanted to order, rather than how many burgers or milkshakes they wanted. As Brannon and Van de Walle (2001) suggested, numbers may not be salient to young children: exact numbers of things do not matter in their lives. The issue is not just about role-play. One teacher from the Number in Early Childhood research group went off enthusiastically from a meeting, determined to record all the times she saw children using numbers in their play (Gifford 1995). She returned disconsolately two weeks later to report that she had not seen a single incident in her large, well-resourced nursery school. Similarly, a New Zealand team (the EMI–4s study, Young-Loveridge *et al.* 1995) spent 70 hours videoing four year olds in nurseries playing independently and found that children used mathematics skills (not just number) just 1.6 per cent of the time. Young (1994), in his nursery study, found one example of children engaging with numbers in play and that was when an adult was at the puzzle table. Munn and Schaffer's (1993) study of ten Scottish nurseries found number learning opportunities were few and, without adult involvement, very rare indeed. Research therefore suggested that children were unlikely to learn about number through independent play. On the other hand, it seemed that children learned a great deal about spatial aspects of mathematics through individual exploration in blockplay (Gura 1992). (See Fig. 0.1.)

Two issues arise from this. Firstly, a laissez-faire approach to children learning maths in the 'secret garden of play' does not work. Opportunities may be there, but children will not necessarily take advantage of them, suggesting that we need to examine more closely when young children are concerned with mathematics and particularly number. Rogers, for instance, found that UK nursery children knew a lot about the numbers on party invitations, and birthday

Figure 0.1 A child's blockplay

party role-play can be productive for mathematics (Cook 1996). We all know children are concerned with numbers as ages, like the nursery child who asked, 'How do you write three and a half?' Children may not easily be able to relate such knowledge and interests to provision in early years settings. The question is, when do children really learn mathematics in early years settings? Evaluation of children's learning from provision is therefore important.

The second issue is that adult involvement is needed to support children's learning. This is particularly true with socially constructed knowledge like number, which is not easily discovered through independent play. However, what kind of adult involvement is appropriate and effective? I found from observation that whole class number rhyme sessions provided the greatest learning opportunities. Like other educators, I found that children enjoyed adult-led games and problems. A lot of teaching and learning went on between children in these sessions. These activities were also voluntary: children were free to come and go, which they did, allowing me to see what engaged children in learning. However, early years colleagues were divided about adult-led mathematics games in the nursery, with many considering them inappropriate. The desirability of adult-initiated activity in early years settings is a matter of ongoing debate.

Official guidance in England has emphasised the adult role in children achieving the Early Learning Goals, which include mathematical objectives. The *Curriculum Guidance for the Foundation Stage* (CGFS, DfEE/QCA 2000: 22) advocates 'systematically helping children to learn' or 'teaching'. This means that practitioners should now be 'teaching mathematics' to three to five year olds, which is quite a change in terminology as well as approach, especially for those of the early childhood tradition. For instance, Bruce and Bartholomew refused to use the word 'teach' because it implied 'adults transmitting, imposing, invading and dominating the child's life' (1993: 14). To them, 'teaching' young children was a practice verging on abuse. For many it implies an adult-directed transmission model of learning, with an 'empty vessel' view of the learner, rather than seeing children as active participants in their own learning. Recent research found that 'the language of "teaching" engenders concern in early years practitioners', and that they have difficulty accepting the role of 'teacher' (Moyles *et al.* 2002: 1). For many it may be associated with 'hothousing' or overpressurising children. Teaching mathematics presents further difficulties, since this is an area of learning which practitioners may not feel confident with (Munn and Schaffer 1993).

It is not clear from official directives what 'teaching mathematics' to young children should look like, which does not help practitioners warm to the idea. English guidance has given mixed messages. The CGFS said: 'Teaching means systematically helping children to learn so that they are helped to make connections in their learning and are actively led forward, as well as helped to reflect on what they have already learned' (DfEE/QCA 2000: 22). This was expanded to include working with parents, planning and assessing, as well as interacting with children and the 'direct teaching of skills and knowledge'. Within the mathematics section, incidental intervention in daily activities and play was emphasised and it was not clear whether adults should be planning focused activities in order to 'directly teach' mathematics. However, the government's National Numeracy Strategy (2002) advocated teacher-directed mathematics focused activities for groups of three to five year olds. English early years practitioners were therefore unclear as to whether appropriate 'teaching' should involve intervening in children's play or leading number activities with groups.

By setting out to teach number to three to five year olds, there is a danger that we could be rushing from the secret garden of play into the hothouse. We do not want to swell the already ample ranks of the mathematically anxious, by using approaches which create failure and loss of confidence. 'Sedentary tasks' and 'the premature use of worksheets' have been criticised as inappropriate and ineffective (HM Chief Inspector of Schools 1993). Certainly, in other countries where they start school at about six or seven, children achieve more highly at mathematics in the longer term, and this has been attributed to the emphasis on 'formal' or written mathematics in England (Aubrey et al. 2000). However, research seems inconclusive as to why children from other countries achieve more. They may learn more mathematics orally and informally in pre-school, as in central European countries (Aubrey 2003). They may also come from cultures where parents have higher expectations (Stevenson et al. 1990). For instance, Korean children perform extremely well in international comparisons (Foxman 1994). I once asked a Korean teacher whether she had learned the Korean method of finger counting, which allows you to add and subtract numbers to 20 by folding fingers down and then unfolding them (Fuson and Kwon 1992). 'Yes,' she replied, 'but I wasn't still doing that by the time I went to school!' This meant she could mentally add and subtract to 20 by the age of six. Korean mothers apparently place a lot of emphasis on spending 'quality time' with preschool children teaching mathematics concepts, which may not be true in England (Lee 1997). It seems that children from mathematically high achieving countries may have a better informal grounding before beginning written mathematics.

The issue of an appropriate mathematics curriculum has therefore concerned many of us involved with early mathematics education over the past few years, prompting curriculum development and observation of children (for instance, Early Childhood Mathematics Group 1997; Gifford et al. 1998; Gifford 2002). What this book aims to do is to draw together some recent research and thinking in order to answer the question, 'What lies between the secret garden and the hothouse?' In this way it is hoped to gain some insights into what appropriate teaching, in its broadest sense, might look like.

What has changed and why?

Firstly, however, it is useful to consider what has changed with regard to recommendations for early maths education and the possible reasons for these changes.

There have been changes in current thinking in three main areas:

- what young children can do mathematically
- objectives for early education
- how children learn.

In all three aspects, practice is now recommended which was criticised very strongly in the past. The tone as well as the message has changed dramatically, particularly with regard to the numerical aspects of mathematics.

What young children can do mathematically

It used to be considered that there was no point in giving children early experiences of counting or numerals, since they would be incapable of understanding numbers, according to Piaget (1952). A major nursery mathematics publication, *Early Mathematical Experiences* (EME, Schools Council 1978), warned against number activities, number books and friezes in the nursery. Instead a pre-number curriculum of logical activities such as 'sorting, ordering and matching' would help children to develop the reasoning necessary to understand numbers (Womack 1993).

Research has challenged this view of young children as mathematically 'unready'. It was discovered that young children could succeed at Piagetian experiments if they were set in more meaningful contexts (Donaldson 1978). The 'sorting, ordering and matching' curriculum has been discredited: Clements (1984) found that it had no effect on four year olds' number understanding, whereas counting did improve their number understanding and also their logical thinking. Aubrey (1993) found that many children could do what was expected in the reception class before they started school. Even three year olds can invent abstract ways of recording numbers and mentally add and subtract small numbers (Hughes 1981). Fuson (1988) claimed that four year olds could count up to 40 and do a lot that is typical of six year olds if they had sufficient practice. This research therefore changed views of young children as mathematical learners and raised expectations, particularly with regard to number. This is reflected in the CGFS (DfEE/QCA 2000), which emphasises counting to ten and practical calculations with small numbers. It does not require children to write numbers, referring only to recognising numerals. Oral and practical objectives such as these seem appropriate, in that they are well within the reach of five year olds and need not overpressurise them. However, the raising of expectations for young children means that practitioners need to know a lot more mathematically.

Mathematical objectives for early education

The introduction of mathematical objectives for learning ran counter to traditional early childhood education views, which held that:

- 'objectives' create more pressure than long term and flexible 'aims'
- cognitive objectives can threaten social, emotional and physical learning
- 'school subjects' are not appropriate for very young children.

Early years education has traditionally emphasised 'activity and experience' rather than the acquisition of skills and knowledge (Hadow, Board of Education 1933: 73). There were warnings against focusing on '. . . the attainment of a specific set of targets. Research points to the importance of a broad range of experiences in developing young children's basic abilities' (Department of Education and Science 1990: 104). The message was that specific targets channel practitioners into ticking these off and losing sight of the bigger picture. So why were 'Desirable Outcomes' and 'Early Learning Goals' considered appropriate in England (School Curriculum and Assessment Authority 1996; DfEE/QCA 2000)?

The poor performance of English children in international tests (Foxman 1994) raised concerns about mathematics, especially regarding lower attainers. There are clear equal opportunities issues: those children who start behind in mathematics stay behind (Young-Loveridge 1991; Starkey *et al.* 2004). Class differences in mathematics between children are maintained in the early years (Hughes 1986; Wright 1994). Ginsburg *et al.* in the USA (1998: 426) argued that 'the developmental seeds of underachievement may be sown before impoverished children enter school' and that pre-school settings and teachers were not supporting children's mathematical development. However, it has also been found that children from disadvantaged backgrounds make the greatest gains from pre-school education and mathematics intervention projects (Sylva and Wiltshire 1993; Starkey *et al.* 2004). It seems that if early years settings do not ensure that children make a good start with mathematics, advantaged children may get this at home anyway, resulting in the 'Matthew effect': 'To those that have, shall be given.'

Cognitive objectives

Cognitive objectives have been seen as an undesirable focus for early years education, and mathematics has been included in this. Tricia David (1998: 63) argued that an emphasis on cognitive outcomes would contribute to 'the shutting down of open systems of learning – death at an early age for the mind'. This rather extreme argument indicated the strength of feeling among early years educators about emphasising numeracy and literacy in the early years. The early childhood tradition has, according to Curtis (1998: 156), 'placed less stress on the development of obvious cognitive skills' and greater emphasis on children's social and emotional development. According to some researchers, this view resulted in a lack of intellectual learning in British nurseries (Eyken 1977; Bruner 1980; Hutt *et al.* 1989). Rather than seeing cognitive aims as threatening social, emotional and physical learning, the issue is, as David also argued, to find ways of teaching numeracy to young children which do not endanger holistic principles.

School subjects

School subjects, such as mathematics, have been seen as developmentally inappropriate for the early years and have been resisted, along with pressures to prepare children for primary school (Blenkin 1994). Number, in particular, has been regarded as too abstract and associated with paper and pencil tasks. Mathematics was sometimes not mentioned at all in recommendations because 'learning is holistic and cannot be compartmentalised' (Early Childhood Education Forum 1998). The general message was to integrate mathematics in everyday experiences and teach it incidentally: 'Always remember. Mathematics should not be split off from everyday life . . . mathematics is everywhere' (Bruce and Meggitt 1996: 394).

However, the integrated approach seems to be problematic. Tizard *et al.* (1988: 33) found that staff were unable to articulate how children would learn mathematics from activities, saying for instance, 'It's unconscious mathematics.' Sometimes practitioners were confused about what the mathematics was, thinking it was colour naming (Kleinberg and Menmuir 1995). Even when practitioners clearly articulated the mathematics aims of activities, their interventions in practice might not reflect these (Stephen and Wilkinson 1999). Mathematical interventions in integrated activities were found to be rare by Munn and Schaffer (1993), who proposed that nursery practitioners' negative attitudes prevented them seeing mathematics activities as pleasurable or informal. This research suggests that objectives might help to give mathematics a higher priority in early years settings, by requiring educators to monitor progress and to know what the steps towards understanding are.

How children learn

Recent thinking about how children learn has emphasised adult involvement. Vygotskian theory has emphasised social contexts and language, with ideas such as learning gradually through apprenticeship (Vygotsky 1986). Interaction with adults and other children clearly enhances children's learning (Bruner 1980). More recent theory has emphasised young children as agents, directing their own learning with adults (see for example, Rogoff 1990). A model of shared learning has emerged, valuing children's control, but with a much stronger role for the adult. Advice for mathematics was for adults to intervene incidentally to extend children's learning: 'The nursery can provide a seedbed for mathematical thinking . . . but . . . the cue must come mainly from the child' (Dowling 1992: 14). However, in educational settings, informal one-to-one interaction may be difficult to achieve in practice. Recent research identified two key components of effective pedagogy as adult intervention in child-initiated play and 'the kind of interaction traditionally associated with the term "teaching" ' (Siraj-Blatchford *et al.* 2002: 12). This suggested that adult-led group activities are a necessary part of effective practice, together with child-initiated activity, as with blockplay.

The early years mathematics curriculum

Recent research and concerns about children's achievement have therefore changed the nature of the early years curriculum for mathematics. Research suggests that 'early numeracy experiences are just as important as are early literacy experiences' (Munn and Schaffer 1993: 76). Ginsburg *et al.* (1998) have argued that knowing more about pre-schoolers' mathematics means that educators can help children more. Official bodies in countries such as the USA, Australia, Canada and New Zealand are now emphasising pre-school mathematics and developing curricula (National Association for the Education of Young Children 2002; Doig *et al.* 2003; Ontario Ministry of Education 2003; Thomas and Tagg 2003). Early mathematics has been the focus of recent pre-school and intervention programmes, for instance in the USA, Australia and the Netherlands, involving adult-led and computer based activities (Van de Rijt and Van Luit 1998; Wright *et al.* 2000; Griffin 2004; Sarama and Clements 2004; Starkey *et al.* 2004).

These changes present considerable challenges to early childhood professionals, as Doig *et al.* point out. Practitioners need to know what mathematics young children might learn and how they might learn it. Currently, more is known about the former than the latter. Rather than debating adult- or child-initiated activity, the issue is now about the quality of adult–child interaction. However, rather than talk about 'pedagogic intervention strategies', it makes sense for early years educators to reclaim the word 'teaching', to include a range of planning, provision and interactive strategies.

This book attempts to consider some current research and issues, in order to identify some principles for an appropriate early years mathematics curriculum and to identify some options between the secret garden and the hothouse. It considers learning from a holistic perspective, including cognitive, emotional, social and physical aspects. It does not claim to offer a meta-analysis of pre-school mathematics programmes, but rather to highlight issues concerning early years settings, of group size, activities, resources, planning and observation, as well as interactive teaching strategies. It draws on the work of many educators who have been concerned with young children learning mathematics. It offers a personal view, drawing on my own research, which included following three children learning mathematics through their five terms in nursery: Siobhan, Alan and Jermaine will make appearances throughout the book along with other children from early years settings. From observing young children's responses to mathematics learning opportunities, it is clear that they do engage with mathematics, they want to learn and they enjoy learning. The children also provide clues as to how practitioners might enjoy teaching mathematics.

The three sections of this book therefore consider:

- how children learn mathematics, from a holistic viewpoint
- issues about teaching mathematics and implications for pre-school settings
- children's learning of different aspects of mathematics and implications for teaching.

SECTION 1
What do we know about how young children learn maths? A holistic approach

Alan and his friend counted the linked elephants which they had joined up into a large circle: with a little licence on the sequence and almost in synchrony they got up to 40. Alan was so excited that he hugged me (which he was not in the habit of doing). It seemed that counting to such a high number, the chanting in time with his friend and the rhythmic pointing all contributed to the excitement. For Alan, the cognitive, social, emotional and physical aspects all combined in what seemed a significant learning experience.

In order to decide how to help young children to learn mathematics, we need to consider how children learn in general. In order to avoid overpressurising children or creating negative attitudes to learning, we need to identify teaching strategies which are appropriate. From a post-modern perspective, there is no single discoverable 'truth' about how children learn (Mac Naughton 2003). However, there is generally some agreement as to key elements and issues. We know that learning is a complex process and that individual children learn in different ways. Many factors are involved, but all young children share developing brains and bodies and are highly influenced by social and cultural experiences. We know that learning is an emotionally charged business, involving excitement but also change and risk to self-esteem. Young children have a developing sense of their complex identities, as children and siblings, and as members of different groups with different practices. We also know quite a lot about how very young children do *not* learn effectively, for instance if they are bored, uncomfortable or anxious, or made to sit still for long periods of time.

By considering current theory and research about how children learn cognitively, emotionally, socially and physically, some principles and issues can be identified in the attempt to find a holistic approach to teaching mathematics in the early years.

1   Cognitive processes

'He's got my counting!' shouted Jeffrey, when Alan threw the same number on the dice as him. So great was Jeffrey's eagerness to remark on this, that he invented a new expression.

When I set out to identify what engaged children in focused number learning opportunities, I had expected to find that it was colourful apparatus or enjoyable physical activity. While it was true that these engaged children initially, they could also be distracting, as when children got carried away with pegging up number tiles. In analysing children's responses to activities, I found that when their attention was focused on numbers, the children were doing things like 'recognising' numbers or 'predicting' how many objects were hidden in a box. There was always an active '*ing*' involved, suggesting that certain kinds of cognitive activity engaged the children. As with Jeffrey's excitement, strong emotions were often involved, such as satisfaction in accomplishment or the thrill of risk taking when predicting. It seemed to me this cognitive-emotional combination 'hooked' the children into number learning opportunities. I identified five main cognitive activities:

1. rehearsing
2. making connections
3. representing and symbolising
4. predicting
5. spotting errors and incongruity.

The activities can be related to the major cognitive processes involved in learning, as identified by research. What we know about these has implications for practice.

What do we know about how children learn cognitively?

Research into young children's learning in general and about mathematics education points to the importance of certain processes, together with children's awareness of them and the learning contexts of problem solving and play.

Learning through observation, instruction, and rehearsal

'I want to count mine again!' declared Alan, playing a game which involved collecting counters. When I considered why children repeatedly counted things or shouted out the names of numerals so emphatically, it seemed they enjoyed practising new skills. Carr (1992) refers to one of children's mathematical purposes as 'rehearsing culturally significant sequences', emphasising the social value of counting. Practice is important for skills to become automatic, releasing mental space to learn new things. In the Froebel Blockplay Project, Gura (1992) identified children rehearsing new building techniques: 'I practised this yesterday,' said one child, showing awareness of the need to do this.

Vygotsky (1986: 188) pointed out that learning is a social process in which 'imitation and instruction play a major role'. With blockplay, three year olds learnt faster in classes with older children who were expert builders, because they observed them. Fuson (1988) found that children learnt to count from watching the television programme *Sesame Street*. She argued that what six year olds typically do is achievable by four year olds: it depends on sheer amount of practice, rather than age and development. Whereas Piaget (1973) stressed that verbal instruction alone would be ineffective, and emphasised readiness for understanding, Vygotsky emphasised the role of experts explaining and demonstrating. With this apprenticeship model of learning, children become familiar with mathematical language, skills and tools before fully understanding ideas. Children may therefore learn by 'joining in' with older siblings who are playing number games or doing homework. A related approach is 'emergent mathematics', where children are seen as immersed in mathematical knowledge as part of their culture, in a non-pressurised way (Stoessinger and Edmunds 1990; Gifford 1997; Worthington and Carruthers 2003).

This implies that we need to provide opportunities for children to learn through observation, instruction and rehearsal.

Making connections and generalising

The development of abstract ideas depends on generalising and identifying the same idea in different examples. For instance, children need to link up the number three as a word, a symbol, a variety of visual and sound images, and with a range of meanings, such as their age. Young children do this intuitively: they enjoy spotting similarities or the same thing repeated, as with Jeffrey above. They suddenly say things like, 'Your button's the same shape as that clock.' I have found that children who are very new English speakers will exclaim 'Same, same!' when spotting the same number or shape. They make connections with home experiences. For example, while playing with a calculator, Jermaine said, 'My mum does this, my mum goes shopping.' They begin to spot patterns: in a nursery with a large 100-square carpet on the wall, children would say, as they went past, 'Look, it goes, 3, 3, 3, 3, 3!' pointing to a column of numbers ending in 3.

Generalising from experience includes the Piagetian idea of assimilation, whereby links are made to new experiences which fit with an existing idea. It follows that the more varied the examples, the greater the depth of understanding. The Effective Teachers of Numeracy research (Askew *et al.* 1997) emphasised making connections between mathematical ideas, such as linking shapes and numbers. The implication is that we need to provide the same idea in a wide variety of forms and contexts if children are not to form limited concepts. Children test the limits of ideas with their own examples, for instance by playing with large numbers or repeatedly arranging shapes. Adults can encourage this exploration of mathematical ideas by asking questions like, 'What if you count in the other direction?' 'How many different patterns can you make with five?' 'What happens if you put them back together again?' 'Can you make a bigger triangle?'

Representing, talking and symbolising

I found that children delighted in recognising numerals and were engrossed by trying to record scores at skittles. They could be creative in representing numbers symbolically, like William, who wrote 'W', I thought for his name: he pointed out that it stood for four, counting the lines of the W (for other examples, see Hughes 1986; Gifford 1997; Worthington and Carruthers 2003). Young children enjoy trying to represent things pictorially, which involves spatial thinking: if children choose to represent a roof by a triangle, they must have identified that both shapes have sloping sides. Representing things is an important learning process, because in order to do so children need to identify key features. Representing may be active and visual, or involve words or symbols. For Vygotsky (1986), language played an important role in the process of abstraction, as a form of symbolising. Children enjoy talking about their experiences and, like Jeffrey, even create new mathematical language.

Visualising is a key aspect of representation which develops before language. Piaget (1947) called the mental image 'internal imitation'. Babies can hold images in the 'mind's eye' and they look harder when what they expect to see is not there (Mix *et al*. 2002). At about two, children develop the ability to symbolise with words, images and pretend play. Hughes (1981) found that young children used visualising to add and subtract small numbers of objects. Bruner (1966) suggested that children represented ideas using 'enactive', then 'ikonic' (pictorial) and 'symbolic' modes. Enactive representation involves actions, echoing Vygotsky's (1978) suggestion that children's first marks were gestures. This may be true with 'finger numbers': Siobhan, who was not strong verbally, often replied using fingers rather than saying a number. Researchers found that some young children responded to number problems by consistently holding up the right number of fingers while saying the wrong answers (Young-Loveridge *et al*. 1995; Jordan *et al*. 2003). It seems that children attach number words to previous images for number, which might be enactive or visual (Ansari and Karmiloff-Smith 2002; Donlan 2003).

Children's ways of representing things are dependent on their experiences. Vygotsky described symbols as 'cultural tools' with which children become gradually familiar in the apprenticeship process. Children therefore need to be encouraged to represent things and express themselves in their own ways and to build a repertoire of physical, visual and auditory images, as well as mathematical vocabulary and symbols.

Predicting prior to feedback

Guessing how many bears are hidden in a box or what shape is hidden behind the screen engages young children. Prediction, rather than random guessing, focuses the attention and involves visualising or using what you already know. Finding out the answer provides feedback, which informs subsequent attempts.

Feedback, 'so the child knows how he is doing', is a key feature of effective learning activities, according to the Oxford Pre-school Project (Bruner, 1980). Formative feedback from adults during activities is important in effective pedagogy (Siraj-Blatchford *et al.* 2002). Children learn from 'having an effect' on their environment, Curtis (1998) concluded from summarising research: for instance, mark making gives children instant feedback. This implies that a range of activities can involve prediction and feedback, including creative activities, as well as mathematical games, puzzles, and computer programs.

Spotting errors, incongruity and misconceptions

Siobhan asked about the nursery number frieze, which started at one 'Why zero not there?' – a good question, identifying a serious omission. I found that children readily corrected their friends' and their own mistakes. They loved correcting the errors made by a teddy 'who needed help with numbers'. On one occasion, a child unwittingly counted, 'One, two, six.' Two other boys unkindly roared with laughter and went on to deliberately miscount themselves – 'One, two, four!' and 'One, two, five!' – with great hilarity. It has been argued that making jokes like this serves to reinforce recently acquired knowledge (Piaget 1951; Chukowsky 1963). Children enjoyed making jokes with incongruously large or small numbers: one child threw a six on the dice and exclaimed, 'A hundred!' and another said her big sister's age was 'One!'

A readiness to spot errors and incongruity is important for revising misconceptions. For instance, young children may think there is more playdough when a lump is divided into bits. Realising that the bits can be reformed into the same lump prompts children to revise their understanding. This process was called 'accommodation' by Piaget (1951) and involved 'cognitive conflict', which he recommended that teachers should promote by providing contradictory evidence and discussion. Kamii (1985) pointed out that this happens in mathematical games, when children correct each other. Curtis (1998) emphasised the effectiveness of 'incongruity, surprise and novelty', which may also cause cognitive conflict. Challenging mathematical misconceptions, by providing varied examples, exposing confusion and modelling errors, is an important teaching strategy according to recent research (Askew and Wiliam 1995). Encouraging children to ask questions like 'What if . . .?' and 'How many different . . .?' helps them to test the boundaries of ideas and pre-empts misconceptions.

One implication is that adults need to know what misconceptions children are likely to have in order to expose these and encourage discussion.

Metacognition or reflecting on thinking

Kathy, aged four, had written 13 on the label for a box. When I asked her if she was going to put 13 things in it, she said, 'You'll have to tell me when to stop!' However, she then successfully counted 13 buttons into her box. Kathy was aware she had to hold the 'stopping number' in her head and talking about this may have helped her. Kathy was involved in 'thinking about thinking' or metacognition, which is another major cognitive process identified by recent research as important to learning. It involves children reflecting on and improving their thinking and learning, as Kathy's comment helped her to remember the number to stop at. Meadows and Cashdan (1988) saw metacognition as children learning to plan and monitor their thinking. Ginsburg and Allardice (1983) argued that children's difficulties with mathematics was due to their lack of 'awareness of executive processes' such as memorisation and calculation strategies.

There have been many developments in recent years about teaching thinking skills (see, for instance, www.thinkingskill.com). 'Thinking skills' have been identified in the National Curriculum (DfEE/QCA 1999: 22) as including 'reasoning, enquiry and creative' thinking skills. Enquiry includes prediction and creative thinking skills include 'looking for alternative innovative outcomes'. Teachers can focus on thinking processes by 'thinking aloud', as well as encouraging children to talk about their methods for solving problems.

Contexts for cognitive learning

Two main kinds of activity which foster cognitive learning have been emphasised by research: these are problem solving and play. These obviously overlap, with problem solving occurring in play, and vice versa.

Problem solving

Problem solving has been generally considered an important context for learning. Piaget (1973: 85) suggested that teachers 'should provide situations which give rise to curiosity and solution seeking in the child'. He saw the spontaneous application of an idea to a new situation as demonstration of true understanding. Problems may be integral to activities, such as puzzles and computer games, or they may arise out of things children want to do, such as making beds for the bears. Problem solving stimulates many cognitive processes, involving talking, prediction and making connections to find solutions. Joint problem solving between expert and novice was seen as a key teaching strategy by Vygotsky, relating to apprenticeship and the adult's role in the 'Zone of Proximal Development and to lead the child to what he could not yet do' (1986: 189). This involves imitation, instruction and rehearsal, as well as metacognition in evaluating solutions and considering different approaches.

Play

Play has an essential role in learning, not only for children but also for the young of all species and for adults (see, for instance, Garvey 1977;

Sylva 1984; Bruce 1991). Play is sometimes categorised as imaginative or exploratory (ludic or epistemic play, Hutt *et al.* 1989). Both of these can involve children in setting themselves problems which involve mathematics, such as creating play areas or props, or making patterns. Children often imitate what they have observed adults doing and use mathematical tools in their imaginative play, for instance with calendars, clocks or money. Exploratory play, such as construction, involves children in spotting similarities and differences and making new connections, for instance by substituting shapes to make other shapes.

Cognitive play can involve pushing the limits of ideas and making novel connections. Alan, playing with the magnetic numerals, declared, 'I've got a hundred million dollars!' which was probably the biggest number he could think of. Daniel, when it was his turn to take away a number of bears from a box, took away none at all, and sat with a big grin on his face. Daniel seemed to have asked himself what other number he could take away and came up with the smallest number he could think of. Elizabeth made a creative connection when she declared, 'My name begins with 3!' as she reversed the wooden numeral to look like 'E'. Lieberman (1977) argued that combinatorial or associative play was part of the creative process at any age and level: Einstein could be described as playing with ideas. Children can therefore be encouraged to play with mathematical ideas by providing open-ended contexts and support in exploring alternative possibilities and new connections.

Implications for the adult role

Some cognitive learning processes benefit from adult support, for instance, in providing varied examples from which children can generalise concepts of number or shape. Teachers are needed to present the errors, incongruities and cognitive conflict which allow children to refine their understanding. Teachers can encourage representation and discussion. They can instruct children in skills and provide a repertoire of language and symbols. They can also encourage children to think about thinking.

Some key mathematics teaching strategies for the early years may therefore be summarised as:

- demonstrating and instructing
- connecting and exploring – providing examples, encouraging children to test ideas
- discussing and using mathematical language
- encouraging representation and visualising
- problem posing, encouraging prediction and giving feedback
- confronting errors and misconceptions
- modelling and encouraging reflection on thinking.

These strategies will be developed further in Chapter 6.

2 Emotional processes

> *Oliver threw eight on the numeral dice and ran to point to the matching number on the frieze, very excited, jumping up and down.*
>
> *Jermaine, after putting the numbers in the right order on the washing line, jumped up and down, his arms held aloft in triumph, shouting 'We did it! We did it!'*
>
> *Dahlia: 'I don't do numbers. Donny does numbers.'*

I was struck by the high level of excitement in children's responses when they did simple things like recognising numerals in a book or counting objects. For instance, when a child threw a dice, typically someone shouted excitedly, 'Number five, he's got number five!' The excitement seemed unrelated to any significance of the number, such as age. Just rehearsing skills seemed enjoyable, providing what Piaget (1951: 162) called 'functional pleasure'. Making connections was another source of satisfaction, moving Oliver to physically jump up and down when he spotted the matching numbers. Siobhan said, 'I had them ones!' when a child threw the same dice number. Like Jeffrey in Chapter 1, she was motivated to find her own way of saying 'the same number'. Successful prediction and problem solving was a source of triumph, as with Jermaine's dance. What seemed to excite the children was learning mathematics and the boost that it gave to their self-esteem.

After Jermaine had successfully worked out the missing number from the washing line, Katy shouted, 'We have to do that game again!

We love that game! We wanna do it again!' I was intrigued by this response, because it was not due to her personal success. It seemed the suspense preceding the solution created a 'cognitive thrill', as Margaret Brown termed it. I was also intrigued that this kind of guessing game was associated with magic: 'You're doing a trick!' a child shouted, as I asked them to shut their eyes while I removed a number. On another occasion, when guessing how many things were hidden in a box, Alan grabbed a plastic cucumber to wave, shouting 'Abracadabra, to make it three!' The theme of magic seemed to remove the risk of failure from the 'pedagogic testing discourse' (Walkerdine 1988). Magic is also associated with the power of knowledge to reveal the identity of hidden things. Suspense, surprise and magic are therefore useful teaching strategies, encouraging children's involvement and curiosity.

Spotting mistakes has obvious emotional pay-offs in enhancing self-esteem. Children find it easier to correct the mistakes of toy animals, rather than adults, and they delight in doing so. Children find making their own deliberate mistakes to be funny, as with the example of the boys miscounting in Chapter 1. Jermaine one day pointed to the number four on the 100-square mat outside, said '91!' and ran off laughing. When I realised I had been the victim of a number joke, I recognised other examples. Alan, who was nearly five, when asked his age, replied, 'I'm nearly four, no I'm nearly six, no I'm nearly seven!' He seemed to be turning a mistake into a joke by deliberately making others and playing with the language pattern. As noted previously, sometimes children's number jokes were based on ludicrously large or small numbers, as with Jermaine's '91'. Chukowsky identified incongruity, or things being 'topsy-turvy', as a source of humour for young children. He argued that their delight in mistakes and reversals underscored their knowledge of the proper order: 'No sooner does (the child) master some idea than he makes of it his toy' (1963: 98). Piaget (1951) argued that children progressed from playing with new ideas to humour. Sometimes children demonstrated creative playfulness, like Daniel who took away no teddies and seemed to regard subtracting zero as a big joke.

This kind of creative humour seems well worth harnessing to promote learning. It also gives some clues about ways to engage young children in learning. Lieberman (1977: 124) described this as 'playfulness' or a 'spontaneous, recombination of elements, joy of mastery and glint in the eye joviality'. Roberts (1995) argued that playfulness should be encouraged with new competences in order to enhance children's self-esteem. Teachers can therefore use playfulness themselves to make deliberate mistakes or by using a puppet to make ludicrous number jokes.

Another aspect of making jokes is about challenging authority, as with the rather taunting way in which Jermaine shouted '91' at me. When I talked to the mothers of three nursery children they all spontaneously reported having number arguments with them. Siobhan contradicted her mother about identifying numerals in a book; Alan argued he did not have ten fingers because two were thumbs and three year old Jermaine maintained he was six. Durkin *et al.* (1986) reported a similar number argument between a young child and his mother, who was encouraging him to count the leaves on a plant. He 'obstreperously' claimed he could only see three, then deliberately miscounted. These reports indicate a mixture of teasing and defiance in the children's manner: they seemed to be resisting the adult power of always being right. Joking allows children to change the 'testing discourse' to one of playfulness, where wrong answers are funny, not failure, and self-esteem is protected. Cohen (1987) contrasted controlling humour, where children use games to deflect criticism and get away with naughtiness, with conceptual humour, or playing with ideas.

Whitehead (1995: 53) suggested that 'subversion' is an intuitive learning strategy, whereby children gain control, both cognitively and socially: 'One of the best ways of getting to understand something is to take it apart and then reassemble it, often with additions and changes that make it your own.' She related this to the idea of academic deconstruction and 'carnival', which involved resisting control, role reversal and time off from good behaviour. Whitehead claimed that 'subversive material and behaviour' had particular appeal for young children: 'No-one needs this kind of help more than small vulnerable children who do not really know what is going on in a world they cannot control' (1995: 54). Young children's playfulness may therefore be linked to feelings of helplessness which prompt them to take control.

The issue of control relates to children's ownership of activities and to their interests and purposes. Rogoff (1990) pointed out that even babies take control of their learning by directing their attention and 'switching off' if disinterested. Children's enthusiasms may involve them in mathematics. Siobhan commented about the frog, 'It got three feet and no tail.' Although incorrect about the number of frog's legs, her interest in animals prompted a number learning opportunity. For children, a major purpose for activities can also be enjoyment, as with mathematics games (Griffiths 1994).

'Dispositions' or 'habits of mind' influence learning, as identified by Katz (1995). For instance, some children when faced with a problem will keep persisting and make numerous attempts: they may keep falling off their bicycle but they keep getting back on. Other children, if at first they don't succeed, will never try again: they have an attitude of 'learned helplessness', whereas the others have 'mastery orientation' (Heyman *et al.* 1992). An important question for practitioners is how such dispositions are acquired: boosting children's confidence and self-esteem is one answer.

Anning and Edwards (1999: 63) suggested that not only dispositions but also children's sense of identity may vary with different areas of learning: 'If a child's identity includes a belief that she is good with numbers . . . she will have a disposition to engage with aspects of mathematics available in the experience provided for her.' I found that the more mathematically confident children came to number focused activities in the nursery. Similarly, Young-Loveridge *et al.* (1995) reported that 'number expert' children spent more time with adults. This suggests that children like Dahlia, who do not have a positive mathematics identity, are unlikely to develop one, unless adults actively intervene. She was actually talking about writing numerals, which I have found produces negative comments and signs of anxiety in young children (Gifford 1995, 2002). McLeod (1992) suggested, with regard to mathematics, that repeated intense emotions create attitudes and eventually beliefs. Another child remarked to me, 'I'm good at counting,' which was partly a result of my telling her so. I now make a habit of telling children this, when they have counted well, in the hope that they will develop positive mathematics identities.

Avoiding anxiety with mathematics seems particularly important in view of the numbers of adults with negative attitudes (Buxton 1981). Ashcraft *et al.* (1998) suggested that mathematics anxiety could be as serious as a learning disability, because anxious thoughts take up working memory space, leaving no room for new information. Young-Loveridge (1991) found that the five year old girl number novices, who were increasingly behind their peers by the age of nine, suffered from feelings of 'hopelessness' and 'despair' about mathematics. This suggests a strong argument for giving children a good start by making them mathematically confident.

Creating an atmosphere where there is no risk to children's self-esteem is therefore particularly important for adult-led mathematics activities. Pollard and Filer (1996: 11) found that some learning situations are 'low key and feel safe, in which the child can feel secure to "give it a try". In the case of others, the stakes are higher and a child's self-esteem may be vulnerable to public critique . . .' Laevers (1993) suggested that an effective learning environment supported children's emotional well-being, and this was evident by 'the degree to which children feel at ease, act spontaneously and show vitality and self-confidence'. He also argued that 'deep level-learning' was only likely to occur when children were totally involved in what they are doing. He devised an 'involvement scale', which was used in the Effective Early Learning Project in the UK in order to assess whether learning was taking place (Pascal and Bertram 1997). It includes attitudes such as concentration, energy, persistence and satisfaction. Monitoring children's emotions during learning opportunities is therefore a key part of teaching and, although most teachers will do this automatically, it is important to value it explicitly.

Implications for the adult role

Sensitive mathematics teaching strategies for young children therefore need to include:

- fostering self-esteem, confidence and a positive mathematical identity
- using suspense, surprise, humour and playfulness
- giving children ownership of goals, choices and a share in control
- relating to children's interests
- avoiding pressure and anxiety
- providing a safe risk-taking environment.

3   Social processes

Joseph's attention wandered one day in a number rhyme session;
his friend Jermaine reached out his hand and gently turned
Joseph's head back to face the teacher.

Human learning presupposes a specific social nature and a pro-
cess by which children grow into the intellectual life of those
around them.

(Vygotsky 1978: 88)

Mathematical learning takes place in relationships with experts at
home and at pre-school: the nature and quality of those relationships
are therefore very important. Jermaine, as Joseph's friend, played a
purposeful role in supporting his number learning. As discussed in
Chapter 2, learning also depends on children's attitudes and interests,
which are linked to their sense of identity, or even multiple identities.
One of Jermaine's identities was that of older brother and teacher to
his siblings and that role seemed to carry over to his friendship with
Joseph. Dahlberg *et al.* (1999: 88) proposed that children's identities
were both fluid and complex: 'Identities are constructed and
reconstructed within specific contexts ... postmodern children are
inscribed in multiple and overlapping identities.' Therefore, children
may have different identities according to family background, class,
ethnic culture, gender and birth order. Sometimes these may seem
contradictory: while they are 'experts' at home teaching younger siblings number rhymes, they may be regarded as 'number novices' at
school.

Belonging to some social groups is associated with mathematical disadvantage. For instance, in the Effective Provision of Pre-school Education (EPPE) study of 3000 pre-school children in the UK, socio-economic status (SES) was particularly significant for number learning (Sammons *et al.* 2002). Studies in the UK, the USA, Australia and New Zealand found that pre-school children from lower class or low income families were disadvantaged mathematically and that differentials between them and middle class children were maintained in the first years of school (Hughes 1986; Young-Loveridge 1991; Wright 1994; Jordan *et al.* 2003). This may be due to a difference between home and school in terms of culture, their 'beliefs, habits and assumed ways of doing things' (Hargreaves and Fullan 1992). Ginsburg and Allardice (1983) found that all young children had robust informal number strategies, but that those from low income families were disadvantaged by the failure of school teaching methods 'to connect new material to what children already understand'. Carraher *et al.* (1985) gave the striking example of Brazilian street trading children, who were very adept at mentally working out prices and giving change. However, with written calculations involving the same numbers in school, they produced ludicrous answers which they maintained were correct.

Lave (1988) argued that what people learn is part of the situation in which it is learnt and their identity in that situation: if school and home practices and identities are very different, children may compartmentalise them rather than make connections. Lave's view of 'situated cognition' suggests that people do not really transfer learning from one situation to another. Young children often demonstrate this in school. For instance, whereas a teacher may provide experiences of sharing with cakes and playdough, children may simply see one activity as about eating and the other as about playdough. Teachers therefore need to spell out connections between contexts and help children to apply learning. As Lerman (2000) put it: 'Learning to transfer across practices is the practice.' Teachers also need to be very knowledgeable about children's home practices, which may be diverse and not very accessible. Jordan *et al.* (2003) found that young children from lower income families did not use their fingers to solve number problems: this is not an obvious association with financial disadvantage.

For some young children, differences between home and school mathematics may not reflect informal learning at home and formality in school. Some children, particularly those from low income families, may lack informal mathematics experiences (Ginsburg *et al.* 1998; Aubrey *et al.* 2003; Starkey *et al.* 2004). For others it may be the reverse. Many parents 'attempt to teach numbers directly and coach children in rehearsal' (Durkin *et al.* 1986: 286), although Bottle (1999) found that parents varied in their ability to do this. I have found that a range of adults may teach counting and writing numbers, including grandmothers, aunts and child-minders. Older siblings are also important teachers of pre-school children, both formally and informally. Jones (1998) found that Somali children were regularly taught rote counting by older siblings in group sessions: their parents had difficulty in understanding the informal, integrated mathematics of the reception classroom.

Young children are sometimes effectively taught more sophisticated mathematics at home. Baker *et al.* (2003) described five year old Aysha, whose parents taught her their traditional method of counting three to each finger, which enabled her to count up to 30 children in her class on two hands. In school she used the less effective method of counting in ones. It is sometimes assumed that if children are taught more advanced or more formal mathematics at home, this will be detrimental to their confidence and understanding, but this may not be true. Three year old Jermaine's mother bought 'dot to dot' workbooks for him to do with his child-minder: Jermaine was advanced in his number skills and understanding, and mathematically keen and confident (Gifford 2002). Parents may therefore have high mathematical expectations which do not prevent their children being taught effectively and sensitively.

We know that children's mathematical competence at the start of school can vary widely (Aubrey 1993, 2003; Sarama and Clements 2004). This need not be related to class or ethnicity. The EPPE study found that, irrespective of SES, number learning was particularly associated with the 'home learning environment' (Sammons *et al.* 2002). This included 'frequent painting and drawing', as well as 'playing with letters and numbers', suggesting that general educational activities might be significant. Young-Loveridge (1989) found that four year old 'number experts' came from families with an 'orientation to number', who discussed numbers frequently. There were similarities between families, in that children played with coins, calculators and dice and had conversations about the time, including using the calendar to count down the days to birthdays or other events. I have found that some parents are particularly creative in finding number learning opportunities. For instance, Jermaine's mother counted down the ten speed humps in their road as they drove home.

On the other hand, some families do not put so much emphasis on learning: Siobhan's mother said, 'I don't expect anything . . . they will catch up eventually.' Siobhan did not notice the door number, referring to the red door: it had not occurred to her mother to point out the number. Young-Loveridge (1989) found that the mothers of number novices hated maths and avoided doing any calculations. Although with Siobhan it was her father rather than her mother who disliked mathematics, parental attitudes to mathematics may be significant. Some parents who want to teach their children mathematics may be unsure of what is appropriate. Alan's mother thought learning to write numerals and letters at the same time would confuse him but gave him sums to do on his fingers: like other parents, she seemed to think in terms of 'school-type' activities. EPPE concluded that parenting schemes in pre-school were one way of affecting children's achievement through the home learning environment. The Basic Skills Agency found that courses which focused on parents' own numeracy, as well as modelling interaction with children in joint sessions, were effective in raising achievement and increasing parental support (Basic Skills Agency 1998). It also seems that a dialogue is needed between carers and educators, so knowledge, expertise and aspirations can be shared both ways.

Factors which affect children's mathematical experiences at home include global changes as well as individual family circumstances. Traditional domestic experiences, such as baking and laying the table, are becoming less common. Even shopping may no longer be familiar to young children, compared with 20 years ago, as parents choose to go to supermarkets without the accompanying stress of young children (Griffiths 2001). Family circumstances may affect the time adults spend with children. The arrival of Alan's baby sister meant that his aunt looked after him more and taught him to write numbers. The diversity and uniqueness of home experiences was also evident in Young-Loveridge's study. One child collected the money in poker games at family gatherings. Another child was very interested in car speeds, time and distance: his family moved frequently and often discussed car journeys. Baker (in press) reported the experiences of Seth, whose father kept pigeons, involving conversations about racing, time and distance, as well as feeding and caring for his own pigeon. Nursery teachers have reported children with particular competences related to home situations. A shopkeeper's daughter played at writing long lists of numbers and adding them up. One child with asthma learned to count 30 puffs with her nebulizer. Another knew the weight in kilos of all the members of her family: her mother went to a slimming club and her baby brother was weighed at the clinic (Gifford 1995). Young children may therefore be part of a wide range of social practices which involve mathematics, which educators need to know about if they are to build on children's experience and expertise.

Gender has long been identified as an issue with girls and mathematics (see, for example, Walkerdine 1989). Young-Loveridge (1991), as mentioned previously, found that five year old girls from low SES families in New Zealand were disproportionately affected by a poor start in number understanding and suggested that this was due to sex role stereotyping and assumptions about the inappropriateness of mathematics for girls. However, recent research indicates that gender differences in mathematics attitudes and achievement are small and decreasing (Gierl and Bisanz 1995; Ma and Kishor 1997; Delgado and Prieto 2004). EPPE found that pre-school girls made more progress in number than boys.

Children may also have their own mathematics culture which influences their learning. Munn (1997) found that young children did not share adult purposes for number, but considered counting as an activity done for its own sake. Carr (1992) suggested that young children had their own social purposes for numbers, which included 'asserting comparative status', 'rehearsing culturally significant sequences and symbols' and 'having fun with numbers' in games and finger play. Carr also suggested that children might initially see numbers, not as amounts but as ages: 'people are measured along a very significant number line and higher numbers are better'. This was certainly true for the child who said, 'Five is an older number than four' (Evans 2002: 67). It is therefore important for educators to consider children's own socio-cultural meanings and purposes for mathematics.

The social relationships in which children learn are also highly influential. (The role of adults and social contexts for learning will be discussed further in Chapter 6.) As mentioned previously, the EMI-4s project suggested that children's confidence with adults might help their learning (Young-Loveridge *et al.* 1995). It also found that the girl 'number novices' tended to be social isolates, suggesting that their lack of social skills might inhibit learning, or vice versa. I found that children often attended voluntary number activities in pairs, where one child was more enthusiastic than the other. This implied that the less confident child would not have come without the encouragement of their friend. Jermaine, as described above, took over his friend Joseph's education in a very determined way. When he taught him to play the Incy Wincy Spider game, Jermaine suddenly adopted a very loud deep voice and an encouraging manner, displaying exaggerated enthusiasm for his scores and ignoring his mistakes.

Jermaine:	Put the spider up there.
Joseph:	[throws one]
Jermaine:	[claps] One!
Joseph:	[throws five, counts] Two, three, eight!
Jermaine:	[after his turn] Come on, your turn!

Jermaine was used to teaching his younger brother and sister at home, and seemed to be adopting a familiar role. Alan's mother described him teaching his baby sister, but he did not reveal this at school. Peer tutoring and learning is important in school settings and this will be discussed in Chapter 6, in relation to group size.

Implications for the adult role

Children's social identities, skills and experiences outside pre-school settings are therefore complexly linked to their learning. In summary, the social processes of learning indicate the need for educators to be aware of:

- children's diverse social identities
- their out of school experiences of mathematics
- their own meanings and social purposes for mathematics
- their social skills with adults and peers.

4   Physical processes

Alan's keyworker was surprised when I told her what he could do mathematically (at four he was a confident counter, well on his way to a good understanding of numbers and symbols to 10). She had no idea, because he spent all his time at nursery outside on the trikes. Alan's family was living in an upstairs flat at the time.

The importance of children's physical activity as part of the learning process has long been recognised. Young children need to engage in gross motor activity and to refine their co-ordination (DfEE/QCA 2000). One implication is that large-scale resources may make mathematics activities more accessible, as found by the EMI-4s project (Young-Loveridge *et al.* 1995). Other implications are the importance of the outdoor environment as a context for learning and the inappropriateness of requiring children to sit for long periods of time (as emphasised by HM Chief Inspector of Schools 1993).

Physical co-ordination plays a large role in children's early mathematical learning, according to Piagetian theory. It suggested children need to internalise and reflect on physical experience in order to build secure abstract concepts. This resulted in an emphasis on practical activity in mathematical learning in the early years. However, Piaget's 'concrete operations' referred to mental activity: children learned, not by handling apparatus, but by visualising and thinking about the practical activity (Piaget 1947).

The stage of children's physical development is important for their learning. EPPE found that children's precise age at school entry, when they were tested, was particularly significant for number learning (Sammons *et al.* 2002). Young children's brains are in the process of growing, so they have limited but increasing mental capacity in terms of working memory (Fayol *et al.* 1998). Younger children literally have less brain space available for keeping several things in mind at once and processing new information, which means they have difficulty with more complex tasks and ideas. For instance, if they have to focus on the mechanics of counting, like Kathy in Chapter 1, then comparing two sets will be too complex. Dickson *et al.* (1984: 18) suggested that children failed at many Piagetian tasks because they were too complex, rather than because the children were incapable of understanding, and that 'the child's increasing capacity to process information' is a more likely explanation. Similarly, Clements (2004) suggested that young children's difficulties with map reading might be due to the amount of information processing involved. Some children may have development problems which particularly affect numerical learning, as with some children born prematurely (Isaacs *et al.* 2001).

More recent research on learning disabilities has also indicated the importance of spatial co-ordination and spatial thinking for mathematics. While good spatial thinking is not essential for mathematical achievement, it seems to provide an alternative to verbal thinking. Males tend to be better at spatial thinking and also at mathematical word problems (Friedman 1995; Delgado and Prieto 2004), suggesting that it is more effective to visualise a problem than to think about the words. Children with poor co-ordination gain inconsistent results from counting objects and therefore form fuzzy concepts for numbers, according to Fayol *et al.* (1998). Similarly, children with dyspraxia, who have poor organisational and spatial skills, have difficulties in checking when learning to count, Bardi *et al.* (1998). Spatial aspects such as distinguishing left from right are also important to mathematical learning. Children with poor spatial abilities may not remember arrangements easily and so may have problems with positions, sequences and patterns. They may also have difficulties in visualising 2D and 3D objects. Children with spatial strengths, often boys, are good at mentally rotating objects and imagining what things will look like from different viewpoints. Other children will need more experience to help them develop spatial skills, but can use meaningful associations, talking and reasoning to support understanding. Children who are stronger spatially than verbally will benefit from practical activity and visual images, which they find easier to remember. Children's physical development is therefore likely to affect their ability to learn mathematics, indicating the need for supportive practice.

Multisensory learning

Young children use all their senses in learning mathematics: for instance, babies apparently detect changes in number with sounds as well as visual images (Kobayashi *et al.* 2004). Children may first use whole body movements to represent things. This relates to the idea of action 'schemas' or spatial behaviour patterns (Athey 1990). Young children seem to develop a repertoire of actions, such as up and down, or round and round, which they repeat and incorporate in models and drawings. (Schemas are discussed further in Chapter 9.) Gestures are important as symbols, as with 'finger numbers' mentioned above. The use of gestalt visual images (Wing 2001) seem to be particularly effective for number, building on children's ability to 'subitise' (or to recognise numbers of things without counting). For example, dice and dominoes help children to remember numbers as visual patterns. Harries (2000) also emphasised sound images: for instance, counting down to zero and then shouting 'Blast-off!' makes counting back-wards more memorable.

Rhythm and music also play an important part in young child-ren's learning. Counting rhythmically helps children to co-ordinate saying one number word for each item. Greenes *et al.* (2004) found that encouraging children to make funny faces or twist their bodies while counting teens or twenties helped them to memorise sequences. It is clear why action songs are effective ways of learning about numbers, with their integration of muscle memory, visual images, language, music and rhythm. Technology, in the form of computers, calculators, tape machines and cameras, can also provide interactive learning with spectacular visual and auditory images. Considering the physical processes of learning therefore has implica-tions beyond just visual, auditory and kinaesthetic modes as recommended in accelerated learning approaches (VAK, Smith 1998). Other senses can also be involved in learning: the National Numeracy Strategy's *Mathematical Activities for the Foundation Stage* includes activities such as counting licks of a lolly and bites out of a biscuit (National Numeracy Strategy 2002). Multisensory teaching and learning strategies can therefore provide ways of compensating for difficulties by building on all the ways young children learn.

Implications for the adult role

The implications are therefore that young children's learning is helped by:

- outdoor activities
- large-scale resources
- actions and gesture
- visual and patterned images
- rhythm and music
- technology and ICT resources.

Summary of Section 1

Cognitive processes

Cognitive processes, which are important for mathematical learning, are summarised as:

- learning through observation, instruction and rehearsal
- making connections and generalising
- representing, talking and symbolising
- predicting prior to feedback
- spotting errors, incongruity and misconceptions
- metacognition – reflecting on thinking.

Therefore, some key mathematics teaching strategies for the early years are:

- demonstrating and instructing
- connecting and exploring – providing examples, encouraging children to test ideas
- discussing and using mathematical language
- encouraging representation and visualising
- problem posing, encouraging prediction and giving feedback
- confronting errors and misconceptions
- modelling and encouraging reflection on thinking.

Emotional processes

Emotional processes of learning suggest that sensitive teaching strategies include:

- fostering self-esteem, confidence and a positive mathematical identity
- using suspense, surprise, humour and playfulness
- allowing children ownership of goals, choices and a share in control of activities
- relating to children's interests
- avoiding pressure and anxiety
- providing safe risk taking.

Social processes

Social processes of learning indicate the need for educators to be aware of children's:

- diverse social identities
- out of school experiences of mathematics
- own meanings and social purposes for mathematics
- social skills with adults and peers.

Physical processes

Physically, young children's learning is helped by multisensory approaches, including:

- large-scale resources
- outdoor activities
- actions and gesture
- visual and patterned images
- rhythm and music
- technology and ICT resources.

SECTION 2
Practical pedagogy

Section 1 summarised what we know about young children's mathematical learning and the processes involved. This section summarises what we know about children learning mathematics in pre-school settings and considers the practical implications for teaching. There are three aspects:

- contexts for learning
- interactive strategies
- teaching systems, including planning, resourcing and assessment.

5 Contexts for learning

Pauline was singing 'Ten little seagulls' with her nursery class, who were flapping their arms and joining in enthusiastically. She decided to throw a challenge for the shopkeeper's daughter who could subtract mentally. After 'nine little seagulls' she sang 'Three flew away!' To her surprise not one but three voices shouted out, 'Six!' The other children carried on flapping and singing.

When Elizabeth said her name 'began with 3', Katy was outraged: 'No! She's four and she goes in the blockplay room and I'm three and I go in the quiet room!' Katy understood how age numbers related to status and the nursery organisation.

What do we know about how children learn mathematics in pre-school settings?

Since the ways in which children learn are complex, involving observation, exploration and instruction, the implication is that they need both open-ended contexts and structured activities for learning mathematics. This was endorsed by the Researching Effective Pedagogy in the Early Years (REPEY) project (Siraj-Blatchford *et al.* 2002: 12). Although this recommended adult interventions in child-initiated play, it noted these were 'not as frequent as they should be', even in the most effective settings. This confirms previous findings with regards to mathematics (Munn and Schaffer 1993; Stephen and Wilkinson 1999). (Gifford 2002). REPEY concluded that children's greatest cognitive progress was related to the quantity and quality of 'adult planned and initiated focused group work', which for mathematics usually involved trained teachers. However, it recommended less emphasis on this for younger children.

Traditionally, both integrated and focused provision have been recommended for learning mathematics in pre-school (Gifford 2002). The first is associated with a 'maths is everywhere' approach, as discussed in the Introduction, including child-initiated play and adult-led activities and routines. Focused provision includes structured apparatus and adult-led number songs and activities. As mentioned previously, recent official recommendations in England have differed in approach, with the *Curriculum Guidance for the Foundation Stage* emphasising focused activities and the National Numeracy Strategy (NNS) (DfEE/QCA 2000; NNS 2002). In the USA, the National Association for the Education of Young Children and the National Council of Teachers of Mathematics (2002, para 9) advocate going beyond 'sporadic, hit or miss mathematics', and various pre-school mathematics programmes have claimed significant results from focused activities (Greenes *et al.* 2004; Griffin 2004; Sarama and Clements 2004; Sophian 2004; Starkey *et al.* 2004). Some key issues concerning 'meaningful' mathematics and group teaching.

Integrated mathematics: child-initiated activity

As discussed in the Introduction, research has repeatedly found that young children do not use much mathematics in independent play (Hutt *et al.* 1989; Young 1994; Griffiths 1995; Young-Loveridge *et al.* 1995; Rogers 1997; Gifford 2002). Whereas shops and fast food outlets have not produced the number learning anticipated, some role-play scenarios have been successful. For instance, a 'plane' produced discussion about control dials and tickets (Gifford 1995), birthday parties encouraged mathematical language (Cook 1996) and a 'library van' stimulated an interest in giving fines (Worthington and Carruthers 2003). Teachers reported a DIY store provoking measurement activity. The provision of mathematical 'tools', including clocks, calendars and appointment books, created discussion about times and dates, echoing Young-Loveridge's (1989) finding that children's home number experiences often involved technology. Children's interests can suggest provision, as with Rogers' findings about party invitations. Creative spatial play has more mathematical potential. The Froebel Blockplay Project reported children making decisions about shape and size when trying to make 'things to fit', like a bed for a bear. Those 'striving to achieve visual harmony' made decisions about position, orientation and pattern (Gura 1992: 59). While it is clear that young children need adult support to extend their play mathematically, research indicates that this is difficult to achieve in practice, which may be due to multiple claims on adults' time and attention or to a lack of priority given to mathematics (Gifford 2002). This suggests that adult-led activity is needed to focus learning.

Integrated mathematics: adult-led activities and routines

'Real life experiences concerned with seeing maths as a tool are considerably more meaningful than the unrelated mathematics activities sometimes offered in school,' argued Edgington (1998: 182). This 'everyday life' approach was criticised by Walkerdine (1988), who identified 'a certain "femaleness" in the very domesticity of the early mathematics curriculum', with its emphasis on cooking and shopping. She found that children had difficulty recognising mathematics 'embedded' in activities, implying that mathematics in these contexts was 'meaningful' to women practitioners, but not necessarily to children. As pointed out previously (Chapter 3), some traditional domestic activities are no longer relevant to children's lives.

It is also not clear that children learn much mathematics from activities such as cooking. I have found children are often more concerned with stirring or the prospect of eating. The practice of skills such as counting may be too brief and the measuring too difficult for children to understand. Isaacs (1930), although committed to children learning through real life mathematics, concluded that most examples, such as measuring on building sites, were too sophisticated for children to understand. She reluctantly adopted Montessori's structured tasks for her school. Munn (1997) found that children needed to have a good understanding of number concepts before they could understand adult purposes for numbers. Young children's lack of spontaneous use of number in role-play supports this. Fuson and Hall (1983) found that children needed to acquire counting skills before they could understand number concepts. This suggests that children need activities to develop skills and understanding, alongside experiencing adult uses of mathematics.

Children's purposes for numbers provide an alternative approach to integrating mathematics, focusing on children's concerns within play provision and daily routines. Carr *et al.* (1991: 2) originally identified children's social purposes for mathematics in nurseries as including:

- ritual – rhymes and countdowns
- status – age, 'higher numbers are better'
- entitlement – turntaking and sharing
- timing – counting 'sleeps' on the calendar
- pattern – painting, drawing or block building
- orderliness – matching, lining up and organising things, tidying away
- literacy – numbers as labels, reading and writing numbers.

Later, Carr (1992) identified that children also have a purpose in learning number skills because they are socially valued. I found that 'numerical celebration' was a possible purpose for children, as in recording basketball scores, which is also connected to establishing 'status'. While it can be problematic to infer purposes and meanings to children, observing ways they use mathematics can suggest learning opportunities.

Daily routines can provide regular practice of mathematics skills at an appropriate level, such as counting the number of children in order to share fruit. In one early years unit, a child would take a number card each day to the cook, to show the number of dinners required; in another nursery school, the administrator would discuss the attendance number with the child who brought the register. Alan's counting of the elephants (Section 1) took place at tidy-up time, providing practice in counting large numbers. Fitting blocks, tools or trikes on to silhouettes can give children experience of distinguishing shapes and rotating them to fit. Setting up routines and organising storage with labels can therefore provide meaningful contexts for mathematics.

Focused provision

The EMI-4s project (Young-Loveridge *et al.* 1995) found that 'mat time' activities with rhymes and stories, outdoor games like skittles and indoor games that children could play independently were easiest for staff to integrate with current practice. I found similar results, and also that adult-led small group activities provided number learning opportunities, especially for four year olds (Gifford 1995, 2002). The issue of mathematics games is discussed below.

Structured apparatus

'There's always a number table, but no-one goes near it!' a nursery inspector told Helen Williams. Number puzzles do not seem to engage children as much as open-ended, structured materials like unit blocks and shapes. I once watched a parent showing their child how to count the pictures on a piece of a number puzzle and then identify the matching numeral. Children who lack such strategies are unlikely to be confident in tackling puzzles, unless an adult is present (Young 1994). A reception teacher introduced a puzzle to the whole class as a game, where they all tried to spot the matching piece: this enabled children to then play independently. Computer programs also provide this kind of activity, for instance, adding pictures to match a numeral. REPEY found computer activities were under-supported, with adults giving technical assistance rather than encouraging thinking.

Number songs and group learning

Number rhymes and songs involve multisensory learning strategies, particularly if there are visual props and children show numbers on their fingers. Usually number songs involve large groups, which are considered less appropriate for young children because they do not cater for individual needs. Tobin *et al.* (1989) argued that early childhood rhetoric emphasised individualised teaching while children actually spent quite a lot of time in pre-schools in groups. Rumbold (Department of Education and Science 1990: 7) advocated planning for groups: 'Young children do, however, have in common certain characteristics which enable educators to plan experiences and activities that can be shared by a group.' Tharp and Gallimore (1988: 78), arguing that individualised teaching was unrealistic in schools, found that groups tended to create 'motivational homogeneity' and positive attitudes. Brown and Palinscar (1989: 410) found that children from some ethnic backgrounds 'prefer activities based on collective rather than individual performance'. Therefore, group activities can provide social support and anonymity, as well as 'safe' situations, which protect children's self-esteem (Pollard and Filer 1996). As the 'Seagulls' example shows, number songs can allow children to participate at a variety of levels in an unpressurised way.

However, group size is an issue: Bruner (1980) and Young-Loveridge *et al.* (1995) found that children were more easily distracted in larger groups (as with Joseph in the previous section) and Tharp and Gallimore (1988) found that teachers' language was more focused on control. Number songs may be more effective as small group activities. Zur and Gelman (2004) found that using flannel board pictures with a song called 'Ten little donuts' (a version of the English 'Five currant buns') encouraged three and four year olds to predict and check. More recently, teachers have used interactive whiteboards to illustrate rhymes.

Pair support

I found that pairs of friends supported each other in groups. Some children, like Alan, joined small group activities with an enthusiastic and more mathematically confident best friend. There were frequent examples of peer tutoring, with children instructing others in playing games, as with Jermaine and Joseph. Chantelle helped another child to count irregular arrangements of pictures on the computer screen by saying, 'Start from the top.' Children usually accepted corrections readily, with number novices benefiting from number expert friends, who also benefited by explaining. Sylva (1984) identified that 'play partners' were effective both cognitively, in articulating processes (as with the child counting irregular arrays above), and emotionally, in giving positive feedback by signalling achievement. The benefits of children playing in friendship pairs and examples of peer teaching have been well documented in the literature (Bruner 1980; Rubin 1980; Robson 1983; Mannigel 1988; Tudge 1992). However, Cobb and

Whitenack (1996) found with older children that the quality of peer tutoring was dependent on their relationship, the opportunities provided by the activity and the level of mathematics. Young-Loveridge (2004) suggested that adults were better at scaffolding and adjusting the level of challenge in activities. The implications are that mathematics focused activities provide more opportunities for mathematical peer tutoring, especially with number expert and novice friends, but adults are needed to ensure the level of difficulty is appropriate.

Games

Although games such as 'ninepins' were recommended by Hadow (Board of Education 1933) and more recently by HMI Inspectors of Schools (1989), games have traditionally been regarded as a poor alternative to creative play and practical activity (Bruce 1991; Pound *et al.* 1992). Piagetian theory argued that young children were too immature to follow rules (Piaget 1951; Garvey 1977). However, Bruner (1980: 204) argued that even babies played games with rules, like 'Peek a boo'. He pointed out that children in Chinese nurseries successfully played games and kept scores. Mannigel (1988) found games were suitable for pre-schoolers so long as they were offered a wide range of dice and 'encouraged to play them in their own way', implying that the rules might not be strictly adhered to. One difficulty for young children with board games is waiting for turns: the New Zealand EMI-4s project's solution was to give each child their own dice and board (Young-Loveridge *et al.* 1995). They also used large-scale resources, such as giant dice, or outdoor tracks which the children jumped along in a continuous circuit, each with their own spinner (see Fig. 5.1).

As well as promoting peer tutoring, games can offer opportunities for problem solving (Hughes 1986; Mannigel 1988; Gifford 2002). Games played with adults have significant effects on five year olds' early number skills (Peters 1998; Aubrey 2003; Young-Loveridge 2004). Games are emphasised in the effective US pre-school programmes mentioned previously. Researchers have argued that games are meaningful and even constitute 'real life' for children. Carr (1992) argued that one of children's social purposes for mathematics was 'having fun with numbers' in games and finger plays, while Griffiths (1994) pointed out that for children a 'clear and significant purpose is

Figure 5.1 Continuous track game

enjoyment'. Games also protect children's self-esteem, because the element of chance shifts the balance of power away from the adult (Young-Loveridge 2004).

I have found that four year olds can teach each other games in pairs. In one early years unit, pairs of children regularly selected a game and then searched for other children who could explain it to them. Five year olds also enjoy developing and creating games. If they are provided with tracks, dice or spinners, counters or coins, they can invent games. Outdoors, children devise simple games with bean-bags, giant dice, number tiles or a number track to jump on, even organising themselves into queues. The aims of such games may be obscure to adults, but they usually involve some connection between a numeral and a number of actions. Games, suitably adapted, therefore provide rich opportunities for mathematical learning.

In summary, it seems that in practice it may be difficult for adults to teach mathematics on a one-to-one basis, or at the right level in integrated activities, suggesting that explicit planning and monitoring is needed to ensure learning in these contexts. Children's mathematical purposes suggest ways of developing everyday provision and routines to provide regular learning opportunities. Number rhymes in large groups can provide differentiated learning, but small groups may be more effective. Friendship pairs provide valuable support, but adults are necessary in order to scaffold learning for individuals. Mathematics focused activities such as games can relate to children's interests and capabilities, provide more learning opportunities and may also help adults to focus mathematically.

6 Interactive teaching strategies

> The teacher was telling a story to a group of nursery 'number experts', aided by some stones in a box and a handbag: 'My name is Susie, and this is my box of treasures. Yesterday, I decided to take some of my treasures out with me in my bag. I thought I'd take three. Then I thought maybe I'd take one more. How many did I have in my bag? Then I met my friend, and she said, "What have you got in your bag? Can I have one?" So how many did I have in my bag then?'
>
> The story proceeds, with a graphic enactment of Susie meeting a gorilla, who also demands a treasure. The children listen raptly, responding by showing numbers with their fingers, and sadly chorusing 'None!' and 'Zero!' at the end.
>
> (Edlin and Hardy 2002)

We know that adult interaction is crucial for developing young children's thinking and learning in pre-school, but what do we know about how to do this with mathematics? Research into effective pedagogy has recommended 'the kind of interaction traditionally associated with the term "teaching" ' (REPEY, Siraj-Blatchford *et al.* 2002). REPEY also found that the best quality learning situations involved 'sustained shared thinking' where two people were focused on trying to understand each other. It identified modelling, open-ended questioning and formative feedback as important, echoing strategies identified in Chapter 1. Research generally has emphasised Vygotskian approaches to teaching, including scaffolding, with emphasis on collaborative apprenticeship and discussion. Other key approaches involve playfulness and giving autonomy.

Scaffolding

REPEY's findings emphasised the importance of scaffolding, which is associated with Vygotsky's emphasis on joint problem solving between expert and novice 'to lead the child to what he could not yet do' in the 'Zone of Proximal Development' (Vygotsky 1986: 189). Although 'scaffolding' is often used loosely, it originally referred to specific strategies to support children in problem solving according to the success of their attempts, by breaking the problem down into smaller and simpler steps and drawing children's attention to key features, gradually transferring responsibility (Wood *et al.* 1976). A key feature is 'contingent teaching', which involves responding according to the child's response (Wood 1988). Mothers seem to adopt this approach intuitively when helping their children to solve puzzles (Saxe *et al.* 1987). An example of scaffolding by Coltman *et al.* (2002) involved children solving problems with solid shapes. Teachers encouraged children to look at the faces of the shapes, which helped them solve problems, and to check they had been successful, with the result that children later adopted the checking strategy, giving themselves feedback. A key aspect with children who had serendipitously solved a problem was helping them to link their successful strategy to the result, which meant they could later use it consciously. Children who just had practical experience, without this teaching, did not learn so effectively.

According to Bliss *et al.* (1996), scaffolding mathematical learning by identifying the steps which would lead to understanding requires good pedagogical subject knowledge, which REPEY identified many practitioners as lacking. Sarama and Clements (2004: 188) found that teachers who were aware of 'learning trajectories' or possible lines of progression were more effective both in teaching small groups and in 'encouraging informal, incidental mathematics at an appropriate and deep level'. Assessing children's understanding, analysing tasks and responding accordingly makes unplanned mathematical scaffolding very demanding, which perhaps explains why it happens rarely. This points to the importance of practitioners knowing how children's learning in specific areas of mathematics might progress, as considered in Section 3.

A group scaffolding approach was developed with older children by Tharp and Gallimore (1988), who argued that individualised scaffolding was not practical with staffing ratios in schools. 'Assisted performance' involved strategies previously identified, such as modelling, instruction, questioning and feedback, and included helping children to generalise by providing varied examples. Brown and Palinscar recommended a group learning approach of 'guided, co-operative learning', where novices:

> ... join in on their own initiative and with seemingly little pressure from adults: they participate at the level they are currently able to perform, or just beyond ... rarely are they called on to perform beyond their capacity; adults do not expose the child's ignorance ... Collaborative learning environments through a nexus of social support, shared goals, modelling and incidental instruction, create new levels of competence in the young.
>
> (Brown and Palinscar 1989: 410)

This follows a Vygotskian unpressurised approach, whereby writing is 'cultivated not imposed' and teaching occurs naturally, in the course of play. Collaborative apprenticeship is a model used by many practitioners working with mixed age groups, for instance in cooking or mathematics games. Since the most effective settings use group teaching, according to REPEY, it seems more efficient to plan flexible support strategies for likely difficulties in collaborative group activities. Sarama and Clements (2004: 186) described how 'increasingly specific hints' had to be 'fine-tuned' for each of their activities, in order to prompt the desired mathematical thinking. This suggests that mathematical scaffolding requires considerable skill and planning.

Questioning

Discussion-based approaches suggest that younger children need subtler strategies. 'A dialogue approach to tutorial teaching' was developed by Meadows and Cashdan (1988: 57), involving 'discussion and instruction followed by reflection'. This encouraged metacognition, including planning and monitoring thinking. Adult strategies included thinking aloud to 'lend consciousness' to children of mental processes, such as considering alternatives. Discussion included 'negotiating meanings' in order to establish understanding, as with 'sustained shared thinking'. The importance of this was shown by an example from an early years unit, where staff were puzzled by their contrasting assessments of sorting. One adult found that all the children could do it and another that none could. The first had used the term 'sort', while the second had asked children to put things that 'go together' in a hoop. Teaching young children often involves saying the same thing in lots of different ways and asking for a practical response in order to check understanding.

Greenes *et al.* (2004: para 3.2) emphasised discussion in their maths programme for four and five year olds: 'Children are encouraged to describe their thinking, and to talk about why they choose different approaches in problems, tasks and games, they are urged to share their opinions and to comment on other children's lines of reasoning.' They also asked children to say what was 'funny' about incorrect examples and how they would 'fix' them. An interesting result of the programme, they claim, as well as higher levels of mathematical thinking, was the development of the language skills of non-native speakers of English.

REPEY found that open-ended questions were associated with better cognitive achievement. Asking 'How could we work it out?' is more likely to stimulate thinking than 'How many are there?' Wood (1991) found that closed questions like this did not produce such high level responses from younger children as statements and speculative remarks, such as 'I wonder why . . .' This echoes Brown and Palinscar's finding that younger children do not like to be 'put on the spot' by questioning. I have found that making comments like 'You've got a lot there!' will prompt children to count more effectively than asking them directly. Saying 'I wonder why' also models and encourages curious, questioning behaviour. Psychology researchers found that young children were much more responsive and successful if a toy animal asked questions rather than an adult, presumably because the child felt empowered rather than threatened (McGarrigle and Donaldson 1974). The implication is that more indirect and less confrontational, conversational strategies are required for younger children. Askew and Wiliam (1995) also reported that statements provoked more discussion than questioning, suggesting that making provocative statements may be particularly useful for teaching mathematics.

The following are examples of questioning strategies:

Closed questions: *What shapes did you use?*
                      How many are there?

Open questions: *Can you tell me about your model/how you play your*
                      game?
                      What do you notice about this pattern/these
                      numbers?

Indirect questions: *I wonder why . . .?*
                      Isn't it strange how . . .?

Statements: *There must be another way of doing this . . . I think*
                      there's 100 elephants in there!
                      What a lot you've got!

Higher order questions:
  Focusing: *What sort of number do you want to make the robot*
                      go further? Is it a bigger or a smaller number?
                      Do you need a flat or a round shape, a straight or a
                      curved piece?

  Explaining: *How did you do that?*
                      Why did you choose that shape?
                      How could you explain to . . .?
                      I wonder what made you think of doing that?

  Predicting: *Can you guess how many/how much/what shape/how*
                      far . . .?

  Speculating: *What would happen if . . . you arranged them differ-*
                      ently/put them together again/did it another way?

Playfulness

A playful style of 'instructional conversation' was found effective
in kindergarten by Tharp and Gallimore (1988). This involved
'deliberate misunderstanding, getting children to instruct'. For
instance, a child might describe how to draw a triangle by saying, 'Do
three lines' and the teacher would draw three wavy lines, encouraging
the child to use more specific mathematical vocabulary, like 'three
straight lines'. They reported that the children readily played along

with the adult's pretence: 'If the child suspected that the teacher really understood, it did not matter, the teacher's response was taken to be playful, and the children immediately engaged in an exchange as if it were a serious situation or at least game-like situation' (Tharp and Gallimore 1988: 140). Young children also engage readily with fantasy, like Susie's treasure story, suggesting this is a powerful teaching strategy. Their response to puppets also seems part of this readiness to suspend disbelief. A teacher described how, when she 'listened' to a puppet whispering instructions in her ear, her entire class of seven year olds craned forward to hear what the puppet was saying. Puppets can also promote attitudes like risk taking. Zoe Rhydderch-Evans (2002: 23) described using a 'grumbling' toy dragon to make suggestions when problem solving. When the dragon's suggestions were unsuccessful, she said, 'Good idea, but it didn't work, you'll have to have another go!' Another teacher, with a teddy who was having trouble counting, said to the nursery class, 'Shall we give teddy a clap, he's tried very hard!' This also demonstrated safe risk taking to the children.

Playfulness, pretence and humour are particularly important for mathematics, where questions with right or wrong answers can expose children to public failure. Tizard and Hughes (1984: 52) described a mother who laughingly accepted her daughter's mistakes: 'This light hearted removal of tension from the situation may be of major help in the learning process.' Tricks and 'teasing' are other strategies which remove tension. One teacher, holding up increasing numbers of fingers for nursery children to name, suddenly held up a lower rather than a higher number. When children called out the wrong number, she exclaimed, 'Ha! I caught you out!' By tricking the children into predicting rather than counting fingers, she turned the activity into a game where she was pleased when they got the wrong answer, reversing normal teacher–pupil expectations. A similar strategy used by practitioners is challenging children by saying 'I bet you can't . . .!' which makes failure normal and success a triumph. (Of course, adults usually choose something which is well within the child's range.) Playfully ludicrous and humorous statements are more likely to provoke a response: for instance, 'I think there are a hundred bears in that box!' Being playful, as discussed earlier, also includes playing with mathematical ideas, such as asking 'What would happen if . . .?' and encouraging children to consider extreme examples, such as irregular shapes, zero or infinity. Playful teaching strategies therefore might include the following:

Joking and teasing:	*'I've got a million elephants in this box!'* *'Are you two?'*
Challenging playfully:	*'I bet you can't . . .'* *'Can you make a bigger . . .?'*
Inept adult:	*'I don't know how to do this. Can anyone help me?'*
Giving wrong responses:	*Giving four counters when asked for five*
Playful misunderstanding:	*'Oh I thought you meant wavy lines'*
Using puppets:	*Making counting errors* *Whispering suggestions*
Modelling misconceptions:	*'I'll have the big half!'*

Playing with ideas and extreme examples, testing boundaries:
'How many different . . .?'
'What if . . .?'

Giving autonomy

Giving children control and choice has been identified as important. In adult-initiated activities, as Dahlberg *et al.* stated (1999: 49): 'It is necessary to take account of the way in which adult power is maintained and used, as well as of the children's resilience and resistance to that power.' Laevers (2000: 27) suggested 'giving autonomy' as a teaching approach, which means: 'Respecting children's sense of initiative by acknowledging their interests; giving them room for experimentation; letting them decide how an activity is performed and when a product is finished, involving them in the setting of rules and the solution of conflicts.' The Effective Early Learning Project (EELP, Pascal and Bertram 1997) included 'autonomy' along with 'sensitivity and stimulation' in their criteria for observing adult intervention. This approach echoes Mannigel's (1988) finding that nursery children need to play mathematics games in their own way. If activities are voluntary, autonomy is assured, as young children leave activities which no longer interest them or are not going their way. With many games and activities, choices can be built in, for instance with number spinners to three, six, ten or beyond. Children can also decide the aim of the game or how to resolve problems. For example, does the person who has most or least counters win? What happens if someone is 'out' – can they start again, or help someone else?

Games can also be devised collaboratively. I once had a set of card 'cakes' with spaces to put 'cherries' on and could not find the game instructions. I asked a group of four year olds how we might play. They suggested taking it in turns to throw a dice, collaboratively finding the matching card and the dice thrower putting on the right number of 'cherries'. I subsequently found the instructions, which involved each child ordering a set of cards. Not only was the children's version at a more appropriate level, the innovative collaborative element reduced the amount of turn-waiting. Children's suggestions can improve activities, as when Ali used a giant numeral dice to show the original number of bears in the box when guessing how many were left. Young children may need to play independently with resources before adults introduce an activity and they may develop their own variations afterwards. Adult-initiated activities can therefore provide creative learning opportunities, as well as giving children ownership and control.

A repertoire of strategies and approaches

A very simple teaching strategy was discovered by Sylva *et al.* (1980), who found that the complexity of children's play was increased by just having an adult nearby. Adults can also be play partners, providing a non-challenging presence or giving encouragement and positive feedback. This suggests that there are a range of approaches and that teachers need a repertoire of interactive teaching strategies, some of which are collaborative, such as REPEY's 'sustained shared thinking' and others which require adults to be more proactive, using strengths such as storytelling. It is clear, however, that these need to be underpinned by knowledge of mathematics if adults are to be able to identify and extend children's learning.

7 Teaching systems: planning and assessment

When researchers asked teachers in New Zealand for estimates of the children's use of mathematical skills in nursery play, these varied from 20% to 80%. After analysing 70 hours of film they found it was 1.6% of the time, and most of this at a very low level.

(Young–Loveridge et al. 1995)

Effective practitioners assess the children's performance to ensure the provision of challenging but achievable performances.

(Siraj-Blatchford et al. 2002: 13)

As the research quoted above shows, practitioners need to be able to observe and assess, and have systems in place to do so, in order to evaluate provision. This evaluation should focus on the mathematical aims of the setting. For instance, if aims are for children to be confident mathematical learners, assessment systems need to monitor attitudes as well as children's skills and understanding. The *Curriculum Guidance for the Foundation Stage* (DfEE/QCA 2000) suggested indicators for assessing positive attitudes to mathematics, such as 'show curiosity about numbers by offering comments or asking questions', 'show interest by sustained construction activity' and 'show confidence . . . by initiating or requesting activities'. (Some official assessment records focus entirely on knowledge and skills, implying other priorities.) The setting's mathematics policy should therefore drive planning, assessment and evaluation systems.

This chapter deals with some issues relating to teaching systems and mathematics. These include:

Planning:
- a mathematically rich environment
- for differentiation, including children with English as an additional language
- observation-led planning.

Assessment:
- techniques and approaches
- some learning stories.

Planning for mathematics

Provision and teaching approaches need to include a balance of open-ended and structured, integrated and focused, child- and adult-led activities. Planning includes resourcing areas and setting up routines which create an ethos and also provide regular experiences which help children rehearse mathematical skills, such as discussing positions or recognising numerals.

A mathematically rich environment

Research has indicated the need for a mathematically rich environment with varied examples of mathematical ideas and multisensory resources, including technology. Basic provision can influence children's experiences in many ways. For instance, if some children prefer to be outside, and most mathematics provision is indoors, they will miss out. However, when the Blockplay Project placed blocks outside, they found that children's constructions spread sideways instead of going up. Rather than building towers out of preference, children may have been constrained by the space indoors.

A mathematically rich environment implies the regular use of mathematics for different purposes. Routines like tidying up provide rehearsal opportunities. For example, containers can have 'stock check labels', showing the number of things that should be inside. If staff 'stock check' with children, this provides regular experiences of counting to high numbers, or of subtraction to work out the number missing. Similarly, providing silhouettes for tools and blocks involves children in recognising 2D images of 3D shapes. Putting number labels on trikes means that children can park them in a numbered bay and also 'book' a turn by taking a matching number card (see Fig. 7.1). Recording the number of children daily and discussing forthcoming events with calendars, clocks and timetables, all build up regular experience of numerals and time. Routines do not have to be dull. For example, one class of five year olds stood up to be counted each morning and were 'knocked down' by a child wielding a large foam hammer. A mathematically rich environment therefore includes a range of regular, integrated or focused activities and resources. The following offers an indicative list (for practical resources and illustrated ideas, see, for instance, BEAM Education 2003).

Figure 7.1   Trike numbers

Incidental resources and routines

- Labels, notices and references: birthday and height charts, calendars, timetables, posters and displays.
- Patterns: from a variety of cultures, on fabric, natural objects, environmental photos, kaleidoscopes and mirrors.
- Measuring tools, containers, scales and timers.
- Role-play: technological appliances (telephones, microwaves, washing machines, alarm clocks, shop tills, thermometers, petrol pumps), references and records (catalogues, recipe and appointment books).
- Books: number stories, songs.
- Outdoor numbers: number labels, tracks, apparatus and games, scoreboards (see Fig. 7.2).
- ICT: cassette players, computer programs, TV programmes, calculators, cameras and scanners, programmable robots and interactive whiteboards.
- Routines: attendance and dinner numbers, calendars, daily events timetable, setting up activities, sharing fruit, tidying up, including silhouettes for tools and blocks, containers labelled with numbers of items.

Figure 7.2 A scoreboard

- Voting for stories, songs or changes to provision, such as role-play areas (see Chapter 8).

Integrated activities, projects and events

- Stories, songs and music, including counting beats and actions.
- Imaginative play: role-play areas and small world resources.
- Sand and water, with containers, things to find or for fishing.
- Construction play, including unit blocks and large-scale resources outdoors.
- Making things: cooking, models.
- Robots: knocking down skittles, following pathways.
- Growing things: measuring beans, hatching eggs.
- Design projects: gardens, role-play areas, giant sculptures, puppets.
- Events: teddy bears' picnics, performances, walks, shopping, visits and visitors.

Focused activities and resources

- Number rhymes, books and stories with props and tapes available for re-enactment.
- Group rehearsal: counting forwards and backwards, in jumps, actions, claps and beats, puppets miscounting, matching fingers to numbers.
- Problem solving: guess the shape, missing number problems, ordering sizes or numbers, visualising ('Shut your eyes and imagine . . . a number of bears/being inside a Smarties tube).
- Activities: feely bags, 'Guess how many's in the jar', making dominoes and patterns with numbers.
- Puzzles and games: posting boxes, shape and number puzzles, card and board games.
- Computer games and puzzles: matching shapes or numerals and pictures.
- Structured resources: unit blocks and sets of shapes (Poleidoblocs, Pattern Blocks), interlocking shapes and cubes, colour rods, Numicon, varied numerals for ordering (wooden, magnetic, clingy, foam), washing lines with numbers, 100-square carpet and matching number tiles.

- Open-ended resources: collections of buttons, jewels, shells, seeds.
- Dice, spinners, counters, coins, number tiles, tracks, boards and containers for making games and activities.

Focused activities can be planned in different ways, either starting with an activity or by observing children's responses to resources. One way is to introduce an activity to a large group or to work with small focused groups and then for children to rehearse and develop activities in independent play. A rhyme or story may be introduced to a whole class and then differentiated with a small group. Children might rehearse 'Five little frogs' independently with an audiotape and magnet board props indoors and with a log and paddling pool outdoors. Alternatively, provision such as small world figures may be set out for independent play, then stories developed with groups of children over a week or two and fed back to the whole group. This allows children time to become familiar with resources and for adults to observe children's responses and plan accordingly.

For adults to intervene mathematically, they need to be clear about learning intentions and assessment indicators, possible difficulties and support strategies, challenges and extensions. Unless these are recorded, practitioners can become confused about the aims of provision. In one setting, children were threading beads: one member of staff thought the activity was about pattern, another colours and a third hand control. Plans with key vocabulary and questions are helpful, such as 'How many altogether' or 'How many will be left?' One nursery school hung key questions from the ceiling above activity areas. Some settings provide time for all staff to plan mathematics teaching for their key group, for instance developing a number rhyme across a week.

Differentiation

Activities may be differentiated for different purposes, according to competence, age or maturity, for bilingual children or those with special learning needs. However, multisensory approaches can provide access to all children. Differentiation may also address children's interests or learning preferences, such as whether they like challenges or being with a particular friend. Different strategies apply with targeted, large group activities or voluntary activities. Targeted activities can offer challenges at an appropriate level for particular children (although others might join and 'play along' in their own way). For instance, Susie's treasure story (Chapter 6) was planned for a group of number experts. With large group activities children will engage at different levels, as with the 'Seagulls' song, where extra challenges also assessed children's competence. Most activities can be planned in this way, with visual aids, practical resources or actions to involve and support children and extension challenges for others, which do not inhibit the less confident.

Voluntary activities require flexible differentiation strategies contingent on children's responses: a range of numbers, resources, activity variations and questions can be planned either to support or to extend. With a shop game, I started with a dotty dice; then the children chose a dice with numerals and dots, going up to ten. Although not all recognised the numerals, some did, and others quickly learnt '10', using the dots and the number frieze nearby to work the others out. However, the different prices confused the children, who seemed to expect three things for three pennies, so I removed the price labels and reintroduced them later. Sometimes children's difficulties are just to do with unfamiliarity and a gradual introduction over a week or two means they can take on challenges.

Children with English as an additional language will benefit from any strategies which include visual aids and non-verbal participation, including ICT. Games and songs with repetitive structures also help children to learn by observing. Choral activities and responses allow children to join in unobtrusively. Mathematically, it may be more effective to support children's learning in their home language, so they are not learning new concepts and a new language at the same time. Children's home languages can be used for resources, including numbers and rhymes, number books, labels and notices. Parents, extended family and friends, teaching assistants, bilingual teachers, community contacts and older children in school can provide support. It is particularly important to consult parents and if possible assess children in their home language: as with Aysha (Baker *et al.* 2003), children may be learning sophisticated mathematics at home. Learning to count is easier in Asian languages, enabling children to have more advanced number learning at a younger age. Parents, carers and other family members can support children at home with songs, rhymes, games, finger plays and counting in their own language or English. They might also discuss mathematics TV programs or support children with computer programs and construction activities.

Observation-led planning

Evaluation and assessment is even more important with new approaches to mathematics teaching, involving practitioners in action research. Recording children's participation in voluntary activities provides evaluative information. Teachers will need to plan activities based on the interests of non-participants. For instance, Thomas seemed to steadfastly avoid all counting opportunities in the nursery. However, he did enjoy the digging patch, and after a conversation about what a lot of worms he had dug up, his teacher invited him to record this on a clipboard. He drew himself and 14 worms, counting up to 11, and then said, '12, 14, 15.' (See Fig. 7.3.)

Finding and collecting things often stimulates an interest in number and might be planned to engage children who, for instance, are interested in catching fish, collecting conkers or finding dinosaurs hidden in the sand. Having clipboards and pens available invites children to record and count. For most children it is possible to identify an interest with mathematical potential of this kind.

Observing what children do with resources can give clues to adjusting and devising activities. For instance, I observed Chantelle putting one elephant in each of the spaces of a track game, which made me realise that this was easier than counting moves along the track. The EMI-4s project came to the same conclusion, devising track games to be filled with counters (Young-Loveridge *et al.* 1995). Similarly, Abby discovered that the little bears matched the spots on giant dominoes, and I realised this could be developed into a group game (see Fig. 7.4).

On another occasion, I put out some different sizes boxes for children to build with, thinking they might use size order to create the tallest tower. The children were more interested in opening the boxes up and, since they were empty, filling them up. This made me think that fitting boxes inside each other might be more engaging. I provided different sized boxes of similar shapes and the children readily made sets of nesting boxes, by ordering boxes of a similar shape. Observing the children's activity therefore led to a more challenging problem involving shape as well as size order.

Thomas B. 25·5·94
4 yrs 5m.

"Thomas in the digging patch."

spade

Thomas dug up 14 worms
He counted up to 11 then 12, 14, 15.

Figure 7.3   Thomas in the digging patch

Sometimes children's activity suggests new mathematical activities. A teacher observing children with large construction blocks outdoors noticed they were walking on them like stepping stones. She put numerals on them and set them out in a scattered way, challenging children to step on them in number order. Some children just stepped and shouted out numbers, while the number experts looked for the next number and some stepped on them in reverse order. This activity proved a flexible mixture of physical and cognitive challenge at different levels.

These examples show how observations can suggest activities. Recurring themes like Pandora's box or symmetry suggest activities which will engage most children. For instance, 'beating the clock' seems hard to resist. Some practitioners are very creative, inventing activities using different tools, like picking up beans with chopsticks or sieving sequins out of the sand. Children's patterns of behaviour may also suggest action schemas, such as enveloping or rotating things, which can be supported to develop mathematical ideas (Chapter 9, Athey 1990).

Some situations, like collecting things, large amounts, patterns and similar shapes, seem to provoke spontaneous mathematical comment about the numbers or shapes. Children's improvement of their physical skills prompts 'numerical celebration', involving the number of jumps or skips. Some activities imply a challenge, for instance matching things with holes, or seeing how much you can fit in a container. Children's interest in themselves and their lives often have a mathematical aspect: activities and discussions can be linked to age, clothes sizes or cars. Sarama and Clements (2004: 183) suggested that early childhood mathematics should be about 'finding the mathematics in and developing the mathematics from, children's

Figure 7.4 Matching bears to dominoes

activity'. Two questions can therefore help in using observation to plan mathematics activities and provision:

- What topics and activities have an intrinsic mathematical aspect and prompt mathematical comment or behaviour? (For example, shapes or patterns, large amounts, making models, comparing sizes, fitting things into spaces, rolling things down slopes.)
- What topics and practical activities engage the children which could be developed mathematically? (For example, matching things, throwing and jumping, shaking things, guessing what's hidden.)

Assessment

Mathematics understanding can be an elusive area to assess, so a repertoire of effective strategies is useful. It is also difficult to assess on a single occasion: gathering information from a range of contexts over time can give a truer picture of children's mathematical potential.

Techniques and approaches

Since young children may not articulate their understanding or be able to record, assessment techniques for mathematics in the early years require some subtlety and skill. Effective strategies include:

- observation
- indirect questioning
- eliciting explanations
- deliberate mistakes
- children's recording
- self-assessment
- talking to parents.

It is important to observe children in a range of contexts, on their own or with others, indoors and outdoors. Children playing games in pairs often correct each other and explain, clearly showing their understanding. Children sometimes reveal more in playful or familiar situations: for instance, the children's number jokes showed their competence and confidence. Varied resources and technology can prompt responses or reveal competence: for instance, children's choice of shapes for a particular model can show what features they are paying attention to.

The indirect questioning strategies discussed in Chapter 6, such as 'wondering' aloud or making provocative statements, can prompt children to talk. Puppets are useful for eliciting explanations, as researchers have found. One child was asked to explain to 'Rabbit' how to count: when asked to do the same thing six months later, and well aware that many children had also explained to Rabbit, he exclaimed, 'Doesn't he understand yet!' (Young-Loveridge 1993). Children's delight in spotting errors can be used by making deliberate mistakes. This is useful for assessing misconceptions, for instance by claiming that an 'upside-down' triangle is not a triangle. The following section gives further examples of misconceptions and difficulties which may arise in particular areas, which help to probe understanding. The provision of clipboards and easels tempts children to record, as with Thomas: in the Blockplay Project children made accurate records of their constructions without being asked, because they saw adults doing this (Gura 1992). Even young children can be involved in self-assessment by asking them how they feel about activities; older children can draw smiley or frowning faces to record their feelings, or record responses to tasks with 'traffic lights', showing green for easy, red for hard and amber for in between. Parents can give information about expertise which might otherwise be undetected, like Aysha's ability to count in threes (Chapter 3).

Some learning stories

To gain a complete picture, it is important to consider the whole child in a range of contexts over time. Carr (2001) proposed the assessment approach of 'learning stories', which involves analysis of sustained observations considering different aspects of learning. These might form part of assessment systems which include observation, focused assessment and information from parents, resulting in longer term learning stories.

For instance, Alan was not readily identified as a number expert, because he was mostly outdoors on a trike, which may have been partly due to living in a flat. Focused assessments revealed that he had a good understanding of numbers to ten and observations showed he used this to check amounts in games. He played with large numbers and made number jokes, indicating confidence and curiosity. His parents said he had lots of number teaching at home, where he taught his baby sister, and he could count to 20. Home information gave clues to his confidence and competence, which might otherwise have been missed. By the age of seven, Alan was successful and confident at school.

Siobhan's story was more complex. She did not recite numbers to three consistently when she left nursery: she did not always start at one, but once she counted to 11. She also queried why the number frieze started at one, asking, 'Why zero not there?' When she was invited to activities she often joined in, but she would rarely come on her own. She was interested in animals and said the frog had 'three legs and no tail', showing an interest in numbers in this context, if inaccurate. She did not consistently name colours. She spent a lot of time just wandering around or sitting on the climbing frame, smiling and looking happy. She did not play with other children: however, when I did observe her with other children, she took things from them or destroyed their constructions. It seemed that Siobhan might have verbal memory problems as well as needing social skills. Her mother said she had not taught her at home, just expecting her to learn in her own time. It therefore seemed that Siobhan was a number novice for a combination of reasons, including lack of experience and difficulty in remembering, but she was interested in numbers and displayed curiosity. When she was six, I asked her what she thought she had learned in nursery. Instead of saying it was about playing as I expected, she said, 'Nursery's just walking about.' Her retrospective self-assessment seemed accurate. At seven she was seriously behind with literacy, but less so with mathematics.

Assessing very young children mathematically can be difficult: in the past we have tended to underestimate what they know. Because there is such a great range in the mathematical learning children bring to school with them, and early experiences are important, it is helpful to know about these early on. As with teaching, more subtle assessment strategies are required with younger children who cannot articulate their understanding. Talking to parents from the outset can be part of an ongoing process of 'sharing child-related information, especially about curriculum and learning aims', as REPEY found in the most effective settings (Siraj-Blatchford *et al.* 2002: 11). Following children's progress in school, while not always possible, can provide insights for evaluation as well as assessment. Most importantly, practitioners need to know what they are looking for and what the next steps for learning might be. This is the focus of Section 3.

SECTION 3
The mathematics curriculum

Identifying opportunities for young children to learn mathematics requires teachers to know what mathematics children might learn. This can be more difficult than it seems, since a lot of what young children are learning seems so obvious to adults that we cannot remember not having known it. We do not remember having to learn that counting is a technique for getting a number of things or that shapes do not balance easily on curved surfaces. We cannot remember what was difficult about learning these things or what helped. In this sense, teaching very young children mathematics requires more knowledge than teaching older ones, where memories of school and common sense can be used.

Research points to the importance of teachers knowing about the concepts, facts and skills of mathematical topics in order to help children to learn and to recognise when they are learning. Teachers also need to know the likely order that children might learn different aspects of number, shape, space and measures, the common difficulties and misconceptions to watch out for and ways of overcoming these. Patterns and problem solving may also be considered as areas of mathematics. Since identifying patterns and relationships is essentially what mathematical understanding involves, this is considered within the different aspects of mathematics. However, problem solving involves distinctive processes and so is discussed here as an area in its own right. This section therefore summarises recent research about young children learning the following:

- Number
- Shape and space
- Measures
- Problem solving.

8   Number

Children should have the opportunity to develop . . . the expect-
ation that numbers can amuse, delight, illuminate and excite.
                                    (New Zealand Ministry of Education 1993: 92)

A group of excited and engrossed children were lying on the floor
around the 100-square carpet in the early years unit, writing
down two digit numbers as their teacher called them out. She said,
'I can't believe I'm doing number dictation with four year olds,
but they won't let me stop!'

It comes as no surprise that the curriculum aim in the first quote is
not British. Traditional guidance had a utilitarian tone, that children
should learn the usefulness of numbers. There was an interesting
contrast with literacy, where aims usually emphasised a love of
books. Perhaps this reflected a mathphobic culture in which 'a love
of numbers' was an inconceivable aim. And yet anyone who has
mentioned the word 'a million' to young children knows how they
giggle overexcitedly. The group in the second quote were clearly
thrilled that they had begun to crack the code for writing big
numbers.

Until recently, it was thought that nursery children should only
deal with numbers up to five, in a 'small numbers for small children'
curriculum, based on assumptions of 'unreadiness' (Walkerdine
1988). Current guidance recommends that 'children enjoy using and
experimenting with numbers, including numbers larger than 10'
(DfEE/QCA 2000: 68).

This does not mean that understanding numbers is easy for

children. It takes a lot of experience before children connect the different aspects of number, as with Kathy in Chapter 1, who wrote 13 on her box but was not confident about counting 13 buttons into it. I was surprised that she found this difficult, as I knew she had counted 20 objects before. However, this task was at the cutting edge on several fronts at once for Kathy. She had to:

- remember the number sequence
- synchronise saying numbers and putting buttons in the box
- remember the 'stop number' of 13.

This is a lot to bear in mind at once, especially for younger children who have a more limited working memory. Kathy was also using numbers in three ways, as numerals, as counting words and as the quantity of buttons. According to Munn (1996: 122), it takes 'sustained practice over a long time scale' to synchronise counting skills and to connect symbols, words and meanings. If adults are to support this process, it helps to know what is involved for children. This chapter therefore considers how children learn to count, understand number symbols and begin to calculate, and suggests some implications for teaching.

How do children learn to count and understand numbers?

The skills and concepts involved in learning to count and understand numbers include varied facilities such as verbal memory, motor co-ordination, spatial perception and symbolising. Individual children may therefore have different strengths and needs for support regarding these.

Reciting the number sequence

> Davinia was crawling and counting methodically along the rows of the 100-square carpet in the garden. She came up to two boys sitting on the seventies and eighties. 'Get out of the way, you guys,' she said. 'Or I'll count you!' The boys hurriedly decamped.

Children learn some number words as soon as they start to talk. Fuson (1988) found that four year olds could count to 40, and some to 100, if they had sufficient practice. When parents told me their four year olds could count to 100, I would think disparagingly, 'But they don't understand what the numbers mean!' Now I feel guilty about not appreciating those parents' efforts in giving their children a confident start with numbers. Munn (1994) found that counting to high numbers and understanding numerals went together: children can usually recite longer sequences of numbers than they understand or can write.

When they start counting, children may use number words in a random sequence, like 'Three, four, seven, five.' Many children count correctly, 'One, two, three,' then say a variable sequence like 'Five, six, ten'. Gradually the correct string gets longer. Gelman and Gallistel (1978) found that some four year olds repeatedly used the same incorrect number sequence. They claimed that children understood a 'stable-order' principle, that counting requires using the same sequence of words, with no repetitions.

If you ask children what comes after five, some have to start from one, while others can count on from five. Fuson (1988) distinguished between children counting 'in strings' and 'chains': the latter can start counting from any number, treating the number sequence as a breakable 'chain' rather than as glued together in a 'string'. Counting on and back is important for learning to add and subtract, as well as developing confidence and flexibility.

Counting to ten requires children to remember a sequence of arbitrary words. The words after ten also seem arbitrary, with no meaningful pattern until 'sixteen, seventeen, eighteen'. It would be more logical to count 'one-teen, two-teen, three-teen, four-teen, five-teen, six-teen'. The written symbols offer confusing clues, with 18 suggesting 'teen-eight'. After 20, the pattern becomes more consistent: 'twenty-one, twenty-two, twenty-three.' However, there is a different pattern in the decade numbers: 'twenty, thirty, forty.' Children commonly get stuck at 29 and may say 'twenty ten, twenty eleven' (Ginsburg 1977). Many children learn the pairs '29, 30' and '39, 40' individually, supported, like Davinia, by a 100-square where these pairs appear together at the ends of the lines. Otherwise children have to dovetail these two patterns together. 'Sixty, seventy, eighty' also sound like 'sixteen, seventeen, eighteen', which can be a problem for children with hearing difficulties.

Although these patterns give clues to the tens-structure of the number system, they are not easy to spot in English. Logically, the decade numbers ought to be 'onety, twoty, threety, fourty', offering the appealing possibility of being 'twoty-one'. For Asian language speakers, counting is much easier, as the same words are repeated after ten: as 'ten-one, ten-two, ten-three'. This also matches the order of the digits, 11, 12, 13. 'Twenty' and 'thirty' are 'two-ten' and 'three-ten', so only ten words are needed to count to a hundred. This means that Korean children, for instance, can count much further than English speakers before they go to school (Fuson and Kwon 1992). The latter need to remember a long sequence of sounds with few clues to their meaning and an inconsistent pattern.

Counting to high numbers is a culturally valued skill, contributing to children's mathematical self-esteem and understanding. Five year olds enjoy the pattern of counting in fives, 'Twenty-five, thirty, thirty-five, forty,' or reciting, 'Two, four, six, eight . . .!' 'Skip counting,' in fives, tens or twos, helps children to learn multiplication facts as well as appreciating number patterns. Everyday counting opportunities are important but can limit children to small numbers or just the class size. However, counting everyone's fingers or toes provides much larger numbers and tidying up, books, displays and collections all provide counting challenges.

Saying one number – one object

Gelman and Gallistel (1978) called this the one-one principle, involving saying one number word for each item. They found that two year olds could do this, even before they used a stable number string, but had trouble in stopping reciting and pointing at the same time. Counting one-to-one is challenging for young children in terms of memory, motor organisation and attention, according to Fuson (1988). She found that telling children to 'Try really hard' helped them to focus on the synchronisation. Rhythmic actions also help (Steffe *et al.* 1981): stepping, jumping or clapping can slow counting into a co-ordinated pattern.

Keeping track of objects counted

'Start from the top,' Chantelle advised a friend, faced with a computer display of randomly arranged dogs. She demonstrated counting from left to right, top to bottom. Children often lose track when counting items arranged in a random array or a circle, missing out items or counting the same things twice. It helps if children separate the counted things from the uncounted, by arranging objects in a row or counting them into a container. Pictures which cannot be moved are harder: children need to mark them or use a tracking system like Chantelle. Three year old children can spot which systems work, if a puppet counts items in different directions or starts from different places, according to Gelman and Gallistel. They concluded that young children understood the 'order-irrelevance principle'. However, Wynn (1990) challenged this, finding that many children did not spot 'correct but unusual' ways of counting. It seems some children may follow taught procedures rigidly without realising that objects can be counted in any order. Geary *et al.* (1992) found that older children with mathematics learning difficulties thought counting from right to left was wrong. Children might therefore explore different ways of counting, to find out which give the same result and why. Counting can be more challenging in different contexts, like counting the corners of a shape hidden in a 'feely' bag, or counting actions and sounds.

Counting numbers, like counting on two from three, is the most difficult form of counting (Steffe *et al.* 1983).

Counting and cardinality

Some young children who have successfully counted a group of objects, when asked, 'So how many are there?' promptly count them again. They seem to interpret the question as a request to perform, not realising that the last number said identifies the quantity of the group. This requires a shift in the meaning of the number words. When numbers are assigned one to each item, they are used in an ordinal sense, to give positions to things in a sequence. When 'five' refers to the whole group, it denotes a 'numerosity' or 'fiveness', which is the cardinal meaning of the number. Ali, having counted four bears, dropped one on the floor and said, 'I've dropped three,' meaning 'bear number three' in the ordinal sense, not three bears. This dual meaning of numbers when counting can be confusing for children, particularly if they do not have an understanding of cardinal values, like the threeness of three.

Some children learn to answer the 'How many?' question with the last counting word without understanding cardinal values (Bruce and Threlfall 2004). It is therefore important that children understand that counting is used to identify 'numerosities'. When Munn (1994) asked four year olds why they counted, they typically said, 'But counting's just saying the words!' Children may just see counting as an activity in its own right, like playing 'Pat a cake.' A useful indicator of understanding is to ask children to get five things from a pile. Children who use counting to do this understand the cardinal meaning of the 'stopping number'. Some children, although they can count one-to-one, just grab a handful, which implies that they do not understand the point of counting. Children can be 'counters' as opposed to 'grabbers' from about three and a half, according to Wynn (1990). With five year olds, Young-Loveridge found that 'counting out' five objects from a larger collection was the best predictor of their mathematical ability at age nine (including interpreting statistics and solving money and time problems). She concluded this was 'a crucial concept for children to develop early if they are later to do well at school' (1991: 61). Munn found that young children have to learn the cardinal values of numbers individually, rather than generalising that the last counting word was the number of the group, as Gelman and Gallistel proposed. Whereas they argued that children's understanding of counting principles, such as cardinality, was developmental, recent research has concluded that it is dependent on experience and the automatisation of counting skills (Fuson 1988; Wynn 1990; Munn 1994; Fluck and Henderson 1996).

Research with older children suggests that a lack of confidence in counting and cardinal understanding causes mathematics learning difficulties (Jordan and Montani 1997). Children who do not count reliably get different results each time and may build fuzzy concepts for numbers (Fayol *et al.* 1998). Not having firm, individual number concepts may prevent them seeing numbers as made up of smaller numbers, the 'part-whole' relationships which help children learn addition facts Resnick (1983). Cowan (2003) reported that only proficient counters were aware that larger numbers result from adding. Children who do not understand that the last counting number refers to the group are unlikely to understand 'counting on' and to rely on 'counting all'. For instance, for 5 + 2, they count five things, then two, then count them all starting from one, rather than counting on from five. Reliance on counting in ones and lack of recall of number facts characterise children with specific learning difficulties in mathematics, but intervention focusing on counting principles and cardinal understanding has been effective, suggesting that some children failed to learn these earlier (Wright *et al.* 2000; Kaufmann *et al.* 2003).

Cardinality also underpins an understanding of multiplication, which relies on counting groups as single items. For instance, some five year olds playing card games can count how many pairs they have, whereas most will count the individual cards.

Cardinal understanding is therefore an important aspect of number for practitioners to teach and monitor in the early years. Children need time to practise counting skills and to learn cardinal values for numbers. They might explore the 'threeness' of three and the 'fourness' of four, for instance by making arrangements with objects as well as counting actions and sounds. 'Counting out' a number of objects from a larger collection is more significant than 'counting reliably', which implies one-to-one counting without necessarily understanding cardinality (see DfEE/QCA 2003: 34). Children can be asked to 'give a number' of things incidentally, or be encouraged to use counting to check they have the right number of things. Nunes and Bryant (1996: 43) emphasised that children needed experience of solving problems, where they could use counting as a 'thinking tool'. For instance, four year olds do not readily use counting to compare two sets, but good counters do if they are shown that counting works (Cowan and Foster 1993). Children's ability to use counting to solve problems is therefore dependent on their counting proficiency, their understanding of cardinality and on teaching.

Conservation and invariance of number

Young children can identify that two lines of objects, matched one-to-one, have the same number, but when one line is stretched out, they tend to say it has more. This is the classic Piagetian test of conservation: the idea that a quantity remains the same, despite changes in appearance, unless some have been added or taken away. According to Piaget (1952), full understanding of number depends on this and is not achieved until seven or eight. However, if this task is changed so a 'naughty teddy' disturbs the lines, children's performance improves; four year olds have been trained to succeed at it (Donaldson 1978; Gelman and Gallistel 1978). The test requires children to use counting to compare two sets, involving advanced skill and understanding. Bryant (1974) found that most four year olds understood 'invariance of number' when one group of objects was rearranged. Some could explain that if none had been added or taken away, then the number must be the same. As Dickson *et al.* (1984) concluded, although children under six generally may not solve conservation tasks, they can solve a range of number problems.

Estimation and relative values

How well children estimate the number of a collection, like guessing 'how many sweets in the jar', can reveal their understanding of number size. With amounts like 15, some children will offer any number over three, saying 'six' or 'a hundred'! Babies can compare amounts with a large difference, like 8 dots and 16 dots (Xu 2003). This approximate comparison ability may explain why some two year olds, unable to count five objects, could say which they would rather have out of four and eight sweets. However, only five year olds could say which they would prefer out of five and eight sweets. Some children, who could count with cardinality, could not say which was larger out of six and seven. Schaeffer *et al.* (1974) concluded that knowing the relative values of numbers was only achieved by five year olds. A more exact knowledge of cardinal numbers is needed when differences are smaller. Adults also take longer to respond when comparing numbers with a smaller difference (Dehaene 2001). So very young children may understand that the later numbers in the counting sequence are larger, but competent counters cannot compare numbers with a difference of one. Apparently, they do not understand that each counting number is one more than the previous one, a principle which underpins the number system. A 'staircase' image of numbers going up in ones can help children realise the significance of number order (see Fig. 8.1).

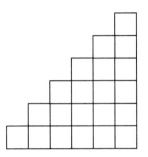

Figure 8.1   Staircase image

Subitising or pattern recognition

Two year olds can recognise up to three objects without counting, which is known as 'subitising'. It was thought that babies could subitise, but recent research such as Xu (2003) has challenged this. It seems that young children have non-verbal images for numbers, which become linked to the number words. Children who could not say the correct number word could put out the correct number of discs (Mix *et al.* 2002; Jordan *et al.* 2003). Children usually learn to recognise standard patterns for larger numbers, such as six dots on a dice. If children can visualise large numbers as made up of smaller numbers, and see six as two threes, they are developing a 'part-whole' understanding of numbers, which can help them to learn number facts in a visual way (see Fig. 8.2).

Payne and Huinker (1993) reported a visual 'part-whole' approach with kindergarten children: this involved, for instance, describing five as 'three and two', 'four and one' or 'two and two and one'. Children subsequently scored better on tests of cardinal number understanding as well as number facts. Young-Loveridge (2002) cited Australian research that aboriginal children who could not count to

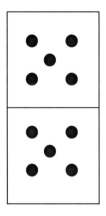

Figure 8.2   Five and five makes ten as a part-whole image

six were able to recognise seven or eight objects. She suggested that they were using visual knowledge of part-whole relationships and argued that thinking about numbers as made up of other numbers was extremely important and should be developed more in the early years.

'Finger numbers' are another example of subitising, with one hand standing for five (Marton and Neuman 1990). This has a kinaesthetic element, so recognising three or five fingers may be associated with muscle memory. Sugarman (1997) reported children splitting numbers between five and ten into 'five and a bit', so that seven is seen as five and two, or eight as five and three, which helped with adding. Numicon apparatus (Wing 2001) presents odd and even images for the numbers, which helps children see that even numbers are 'doubles' which can be halved, supporting later learning of multiplication and division (see Fig. 8.3).

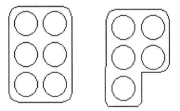

Figure 8.3   Numicon images for five and six

Fuson and Hall (1983) pointed out that mathematics educators had neglected children's capacity for auditory subitising, or recognising a number of sounds. Babies apparently discriminate numbers by sound (Kobayashi *et al.* 2004). This suggests that sound patterns and music, as well as number rhymes, can support number learning. Subitising in a variety of modes therefore has great potential to help children learn cardinal concepts and number facts, building on non-verbal strengths.

Number symbols

I found that children became excited when they recognised numerals. Numerals may be easier to read than words because they are logographs: one symbol stands for one word, whereas a written word has several symbols. Young children can create their own number symbols, as illustrated in Fig. 8.4.

Contrary to Piagetian ideas that young children do not understand abstract symbols, Hughes (1986) found that three year olds intuitively used an abstract tallying system. Many number systems around the world use tallies for the first few numbers: 2 and 3 can be seen as two and three lines, joined up. However, some children have difficulty understanding that one symbol can stand for four things. For example, Munn (1994) found that some four year olds wrote 1234 instead of 4, presumably thinking they needed four numbers to stand for four.

Munn found that children's understanding of conventional numerals was related to their counting and understanding of cardinality. She developed a variation of Hughes' 'Tins game', where children put labels on boxes to show the number of blocks inside. I played this with Jermaine. After he had correctly written numbers on labels, he shut his eyes while a teddy secretly added a block to one of the boxes: he then had to find where it had been hidden. He read 'Two' on the label of a box, opened it and said 'Three' for the number of blocks inside. When I asked, 'So where has the teddy hidden the block?' he replied, 'I don't know!' Like Munn, I found that children used a range of strategies, like shaking the boxes, or watching my face while they picked up the boxes to see if my expression gave the game away. This implied they did not really understand the cardinal meaning of numerals. Munn found that children who could write symbols were better at understanding their function. Children who were 'counters' rather than 'grabbers' were also more likely to be successful. However,

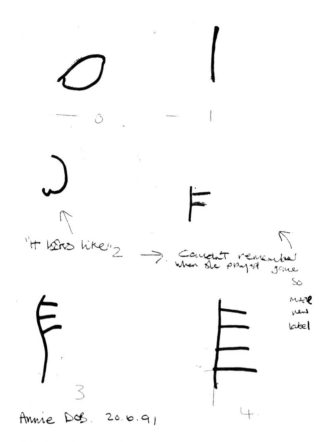

Figure 8.4 A child's invented numerals

children who used their own marks could not interpret them in this context. Brizuela (2004) found that both children's invented recording and standard symbols helped their understanding. Encouraging children to record numbers in their own way can also show when they start to use numerals with understanding.

Some children may understand numerals but lack the fine motor skills to write them. Recommendations such as the *Curriculum Guidance for the Foundation Stage* (DfEE/QCA 2000) emphasise practical and oral activity and do not require children to form numerals. Pressure to write numerals can cause stress for some children (Gifford

1995). Numeral writing can be practised as a gross motor action initially, for instance with large paintbrushes or chalk outdoors. Magnetic, wooden, plastic or carpet numerals can be used in activities so that children select numerals rather than having to write them.

Different meanings for numbers: cardinal, ordinal, codes and measures

The '6' on a box of eggs is a rare everyday example of a number symbol with a cardinal meaning. (Other examples are multipacks of crisps or chocolate bars, where numerals show how many are inside.) Numerals in everyday life are often used as codes, as on telephones and cars, rather than referring to a number of things: the number seven bus does not have seven people or seven wheels. Numerals are sometimes used ordinally, to identify positions, as with house or page numbers. Research suggests that the ordinal vocabulary 'first, second, third' is not relevant to young children. For example, Bruce and Threllfall (2004) found that no children out of 90 pre-schoolers understood the word 'third'.

When adults count children aloud, child number three invariably shouts indignantly, 'I'm not three, I'm four!' assuming that the numbers denote age. Numbers used in this way are measures, as with speed signs, height charts, prices and clocks, and refer to units, such as miles per hour, pounds or hours. Young children have great difficulty appreciating what these refer to (Fuson and Hall 1983). Although the most significant number for young children is their age, a four year old can have no idea of what a year is. Hence children seem to give their own meaning to 'being four' and see the number as a kind of identity tag or status symbol (Carr 1992).

Munn (1994) emphasised that assigning cardinal meanings to individual numerals was a slow process, while Fuson and Hall (1983) concluded that it takes children a long time to join up the different meanings for numbers. Experiences which build on everyday uses of numerals will promote familiarity and confidence in numeral recognition. Children also need experiences which relate numerals to their cardinal values, suggesting the importance of number friezes, books, displays and collecting games with numeral dice. Number lines illustrated with dots or pictures will help children link ordinal and cardinal meanings for numbers (see Fig. 8.5).

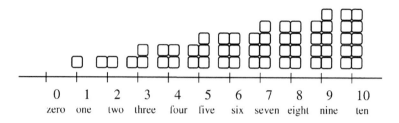

Figure 8.5 A number line with number values

How do children begin to calculate?

> The teacher had put one spoonful of flour into the cooking
> bowl and the recipe said two were needed. She asked four
> year old Kelly, a number expert, 'How many more do we
> need?' Kelly replied firmly, 'Two,' despite repetition and
> explanations.

When children begin to solve number problems in practical contexts,
they come across different kinds of addition and subtraction situations. For instance, adding can involve putting two groups together
or adding more on to one group. Different practical situations will
involve different vocabulary: 'taking away' can involve 'eating' or
'giving' or 'being absent' and teachers need to help children connect
all these situations. Subtractions like 5 – 2 can refer to 'taking away'
two from five or 'finding the difference between' five and two.
Answering difference questions like 'How many more?' is much more
difficult (Dickson *et al.* 1984). Young children, like Kelly, seem to
assume the adult was trying to say, 'Which number is more?'

Children begin to calculate with objects, but researchers such as
Hughes (1986) found that three year olds could solve hypothetical
problems, such as 'What is one sweet and two sweets?' This was an
important finding, because it implied that young children can work
with images and do not need concrete objects to calculate. However,
four year olds could not solve abstract number problems like 'How
many is three and one more?' Hughes found that using fingers helped
children bridge between concrete and abstract. I have found that
young children readily use fingers to demonstrate doubles facts, like
'two and two' and 'three and three'. Children from Asian cultures

may have skilful ways of calculating with fingers, as with Aysha (Chapter 3, Baker *et al.* 2003). Her father used his thumb to count three to a finger and showed six by folding over two fingers: so Aysha might see six as two threes and might soon be thinking in threes.

Children's strategies for adding usually progress from 'counting all' to 'counting on', as described above. Although some four year olds may discover 'counting on', other children may not do this before six (Groen and Resnick 1977; Carpenter and Moser 1984). Children can be taught to count on by covering up the first group of objects. Some children, when the first group is covered up, seem to visualise the objects, pointing to where they would be under the cover. If all the objects are visible, children tend to revert to 'counting all' (Fuson 1988). This suggests that children take time to become confident with strategies, but using blocks may encourage reliance on counting in ones. An even more advanced strategy is to 'count on from the larger' number: with six add nine, it is more efficient to count on from nine. This involves realising that reversing the order does not affect the total, which is the commutative property of addition.

Young children can begin to recall addition facts like 'two and one more' or 'two and two'. Usually children first learn to add or subtract one or two, then the doubles and number bonds for smaller totals (Cowan 2003). Some children quickly learn that 'one more' is the next counting number and 'one less' is the next number counting backwards, without necessarily using this language. Children often ask for more but seldom for less, as Walkerdine (1988) pointed out. I have found that a useful assessment is to say you are giving children five pennies but only give four: they can often tell you that they need one more. If you give them six, some may even tell you to take one back. This occasion often arises when children check their own counting in games. Knowing that 'one missing' can be corrected by 'one more' also shows understanding of 'inverse operations', that addition and subtraction reverse each other. With a 'staircase' of numbers made with interlocking cubes, children can reorder muddled rods or find the missing one.

Mental calculation strategies

Quite young children use mental strategies to solve problems in a practical context. A game which encourages this is Hughes' (1986)

'Box game': for instance, three teddies are put in a box, then one is removed, and children say how many are still in the box. Some children will say 'One,' because that is the number they can see, but others will know there are two, either by visualising or because they know that one less than three is two. Very young children can play this game and show the answer on their fingers. Some children may begin to calculate by using fingers to stand for objects. Lianne solved the problem of five counters in the box and three taken out by matching the three counters to three fingers and counting the remaining two fingers. This was a creative strategy, taking advantage of the number five. Some children will progress from using to visualising fingers.

In a reception class where they had a lot of practice in visualising and using fingers, some four year olds were asked to explain their strategies with this activity. They were used to doing things like 'Shut your eyes and imagine four bears, then another one comes' and 'Show me four fingers on two hands. Now show me four fingers another way.' The children were doing the activity individually, using little plastic bears and a small box with a lid. These were a very competent and articulate group of four year olds, supporting Hughes' finding that middle class pre-schoolers might be a year ahead of less advantaged peers, irrespective of nursery school experience. More importantly, they show children making the transition between visualising objects and treating numbers abstractly, as well as using strategies creatively.

Hazel: [Four bears in the box and four added: 4 + 4] I counted four then another four: that makes eight. Listen to me: one, two, three, four (pause), five, six, seven, eight.

Hazel counted numbers as items, the most abstract form of counting, using a verbal 'count all' strategy. She was also clearly aware of what thinking strategies she had used.

Hazel: [4 – 2] How many did we have?
Pauline: Four.
Hazel: Two and two make four. Two.

Here, she recalled an abstract addition fact, a double, and used this to solve the subtraction problem, showing understanding of inverse operations.

Hazel: [7 – 3] Four. I went seven, six, five, four.

Hazel used counting back effectively. This is quite demanding: she could keep track of how many back she had counted. Another child did the same calculation using this strategy and initially got the answer three:

Aislinn: I counted five, four, three instead of six, five, four!

Not only could Aislinn correct herself, but she was also able to describe what went wrong, showing an impressive awareness of her mental strategies.

Hazel: [6 – 2] I'm trying to think. [Sits quietly thinking] We took five and six out didn't we? Four.

Here, Hazel seemed to be visualising the bears numbered in order. This 'bear number line' seemed to bridge between visualising objects and counting on and back, helping her work with larger numbers. Overall, Hazel demonstrated a repertoire of strategies, including visualising, using number facts and counting forwards and backwards. She also confidently switched between strategies: this flexibility and creativity is typical of higher attaining children (Askew and Wiliam 1995).

Daniel, also four, seemed to deal with abstract numbers, rather than imagining bears:

Daniel: Seven bears in the box and one taken out. [7 – 1] Six: one two three, one two three. Cause three and three make six. When I see six, I see three and three.

Daniel recalled the answer but also seemed to visualise the dice pattern for six. He went on to set his own numbers, removing five each time:

Daniel: [13 – 5] Eight. Let's have 14. Last time it was eight so now it has to be nine.

Here, Daniel was using reasoning, implicitly generalising a rule of 'increase the starting number by one, take away the same number and the result will increase by one'. This is extremely impressive for a young child. This is also an example of a 'derived fact' strategy, which uses a known fact to work out a new one: another example is working out 5 + 6 from 5 + 5.

This activity, which is advocated in pre-school mathematics programmes (see, for example, Griffin 2004; Sarama and Clements 2004), demonstrates how practical activities can challenge high achievers in pre-school settings, without resorting to written calculations. It is also an example of how a teacher-directed activity can develop into an investigation controlled by the child, allowing them to be creative and discover number patterns. Children can also play this as a game in pairs, rehearsing and becoming confident with the number bonds involved. It has many variations, with counters in pots, beans under a cloth, dinosaurs in caves or children hidden behind a screen. It involves children in several of the key cognitive learning processes identified earlier. Children were making connections and generalising by devising strategies and spotting patterns. They were applying their counting skills, using mathematical language, representing and visualising, spotting errors, predicting and problem solving, as well as articulating processes.

Operator signs and equations

Around the world there appears to be a consensus that the introduction of written 'sums' or equations for children under six is not appropriate. Children from countries where they start school later overtake English children in their mathematical understanding. The implication is that it is the early emphasis on written arithmetic which is detrimental to children's mathematics (Aubrey *et al.* 2000). It may be that other factors, such as parental attitudes to mathematics, are influential. However, research indicates that oral, mental and practical games and activities are more likely to help children develop a feeling for number. These are usually recommended for kindergarten programmes, including those provided for disadvantaged children (Starkey *et al.* 2004).

Hughes (1986) asked 90 five to seven year olds to record the box game and none did so with equations. Although they did 'sums' regularly, they did not connect these with the practical activity: instead they drew arrows and hands. Signs like + and – may seem too static to represent the practical actions of adding and taking away: gestures may be more appropriate (Dufour-Janvier *et al.* 1987). I have found that six year olds spontaneously use letters instead of signs, such as 'm' for 'more' and 'p' for 'plus'. Young children have particular difficulty with understanding the equation format of 'sums' and the = sign. They may treat the signs like punctuation, to keep numbers apart. Charlotte, recording two bears and one more, wrote '2' and '3', focusing on the total. However, she then decided to put '+' in between 2 and 3 and then wrote '=', saying, 'then you've got to plus it!' Children often see the equals sign as a trigger for action, referring to it as 'plus' (Gifford 1990, 1997). However, as Ginsburg and Baron (1993) pointed out, the equals sign indicates equivalence and to really understand it children should be able to write equations like $2 + 3 = 4 + 1$, and solve $? = 2 + 3$, which is challenging for seven year olds.

Young children may enjoy sitting with older siblings doing 'sums'. It is also possible to train children to do 'sums' by counting objects. Hughes (1986) found that children could be taught to use magnetic plus and minus signs with understanding in games. However, informal mathematics recording is generally recommended for younger children: although not commonly seen, it can be very informative for teachers. Children may even invent their own symbols, such as a vertical line for 'difference' (Gifford 1990). Worthington and Carruthers (2003) have reported similar and varied examples. Five year olds can be asked to 'put something on paper' to show parents or the teacher what they have been doing, providing a purpose for recording a game or activity, after they have become confident practically.

Place value: written numbers over ten

It makes sense to build on young children's interest in large numbers. I have found that four year olds often refer to a million; some know that it has six zeros and can write it on the calculator (Gifford 1995). However, as discussed above, reading and writing numbers 10 to 20 is very confusing and it may take children a long time to learn these. A display with images of 10 and one, 10 and two and so on can help children decode the numerals. Young-Loveridge (2002) found that using one dozen egg-boxes cut down to make 'tens frames' (see Fig. 8.5) helped children understand why 10 and 3 made 13. Partitioning numbers over 10 will also help children gain familiarity with these numbers.

Young children can learn to read and write two-digit numbers to 100. Brizuela (2004) described a child who explained that the 3 in 31 was pronounced 30 and not 'three', because it was a 'capital' 3. Similarly, 4 in 46 was a 'capital' 4 and pronounced 40. She had made sense of the number names drawing on her literacy knowledge, rather than number values. However, young children will take some time to understand the place value system and to realise that in two-digit numbers, the left hand digit refers to tens. For children who confuse left and right, it is not obvious that there are three tens in 31 and three ones in 13. Four year old Chantelle wrote the biggest number she knew, 'a hundred and one', as '1001'. Very logically, Chantelle had assumed that if you put together the symbols for a hundred and for one, you would write a hundred and one. Young children often make this error when they try to write numbers over 20, and write 201 for 21. Thompson (2000) advocated explaining 21 as 'twenty and one', rather than explaining 21 as 'two tens and one'. He argued that the 'quantity value', rather than the 'column value', helped children to understand place value. 'Twenty,' the quantity value, is more meaningful for children than 'two tens'. Overlapping place value cards with '20' and '1' helps children to see how the number is made up (see Fig. 8.6).

Figure 8.6   Place value cards

The four year olds who were writing two-digit numbers also had a giant number track outdoors which they could jump along and count. Number lines, squares and tracks, indoors and outdoors, can help promote confidence with large numbers.

The beginnings of multiplication and division

As mentioned previously, some young children can count pairs: counting groups of the same number is the basis of multiplication. Teachers may sometimes ask children to get into groups of two or three for activities. Making groups of the same number also underpins the 'grouping' aspect of division. Practical problem solving involving grouping and sharing therefore provides children with a foundation for later learning.

Number provision and activities related to learning processes

A varied combination of provision and activities can give children experience of a range of processes involved in becoming confident with number.

A numeracy rich environment

As described in Chapter 7, providing children with experience of a range of numbers used in a variety of contexts helps them to become familiar with uses for number and to make connections between these. The role of adults is therefore to help children learn the meanings for number words and symbols and to see them as things to think and play with. This provides opportunities for imitation and rehearsal.

Counting for a purpose

Counting cardinally, 'to find the many', seems to occur in three main contexts in early years settings: preparing, checking and comparing. Preparing involves getting the right number of things for people doing an activity or laying a table. Checking involves counting numbers of children at the beginning of the day and seeing whether pens, scissors or counters have got lost at tidy-up time. Comparing involves sharing things out fairly, so everyone has the same. The beginnings and ends of activities therefore offer rich possibilities for number learning, including adults modelling and reflecting on processes, making connections between numbers used in different situations, as well as problem solving and communicating.

Counting to high numbers

Counting collections of things (shells, buttons and leaves), very small things (sequins, jewels, beans and seeds), displays (stars, wrapping paper or computer created patterns) 100-square carpets and long number lines or tracks outdoors provide opportunities for children to rehearse skills and develop confidence in an unpressurised way.

Cross-curricular contexts and data handling

Lots of contexts for counting, cooking or growing will involve measures like time (see Chapter 10). Sometimes children may be interested in data handling and surveys about favourite pets or local traffic, although very young children are less likely to be interested in the views of the majority or general trends. However, when such surveys are related to issues which affect them, they are more interested. Children in one nursery were engaged by the question, 'Do the boys hog the trikes?' and so collected data to investigate this, by tallying boys and girls. Voting is motivating for younger children: it may involve daily events, like which book to read, song to sing or game to play at the end of the session, or which flavour cakes or drinks to make. Children can vote by choosing pictures or objects, or with name cards, arranged in columns next to the appropriate book or illustrated label (for more ideas, see Baratta-Lorton 1976). However, young children may have difficulty understanding why the option they have not voted for gets chosen, providing an early experience of citizenship. Asking children to predict results will engage them further and provide valuable insights into their estimation and reasoning skills, as well as their empathetic understanding. Other cross-curricular opportunities include:

- Physical development – counting developing skills, for example, how many hops, bounces, skips, goals or catches you can do, then how many in a minute; how many times round the obstacle course or training circuit.
- Making things – how many parts you need, for example, how many wheels for your bus.
- Pattern making – for example, symmetrical patterns which require counting to make sure both sides are the same.

These opportunities will involve rehearsal, making connections between different contexts, problem solving and predicting, as well as communicating and representing in different ways.

Numerals around

Jermaine said, 'I've got 5 on my TV at home.' Paula, age five, had learned the numerals 1–12 from the clockface, knew 100 from a number book and 34, which was her mother's age, from the TV channels (Brizuela 2004). Familiar things with numbers on, like scales, telephones, money, timetables, calendars, clocks, dials, tickets, televisions, microwaves, calculators and computers, help children relate to home experiences. Photos and displays of numbers in the environment can stimulate discussion or the making of signs, such as speed signs. Numerals also need to be available as references, for when children want to make a birthday card or party invitation. Friezes with illustrated numerals and dice with numerals and dots help children to decode the symbols. Portable numerals can be used to celebrate achievements or label collections, indoors or out (see Fig. 8.7).

Figure 8.7 Numerals for labelling collections

Numbers can be used on signs or as labels on trikes, chairs or doors. One nursery reported that putting numerals on the toilet doors promoted number talk. Numbers outdoors can be huge, painted on walls or on the ground, or on apparatus, for throwing at or jumping on. Large paintbrushes, chalk, easels and clipboards will encourage number recording. Children will also be involved in rehearsing and imitating adults, talking and making connections.

Numerals and cardinality

Numerals referring to a number of things are rare in the environment, although some settings have labels that indicate how many children are allowed to play in an area, usually provoking discussion about subtraction in the number of children to be expelled. In some settings, children complete a daily 'who's here' chart or take the register to an administrator who discusses the number present that day. In one unit, a child took a number card to the cook to show how many dinners were required that day. As mentioned previously, 'stock check' labels on containers promote discussion about the number of items missing at tidy-up time, involving subtraction as well as counting. Recipe cards can indicate numbers of spoons, cups or eggs with pictures. One nursery had an office area with a large box as a photocopier, where children pressed a numeral 'button' to indicate the number of copies while a child inside the box passed them out. Again, children will be rehearsing and imitating adults, talking and making connections.

Number rhymes, stories and group time activities

Rhymes can provide experience of numbers at all levels. Children can rehearse the number sequence and link number names with numbers of objects. Children can hold up numerals to make the link with symbols. Most traditional rhymes deal with subtraction; a few, like 'An elephant came out to play' (Thatcher 1998) have an addition pattern of 'one more'. Children can be encouraged to predict the next number or you could add or subtract two. Finger patterns can be rehearsed alongside number rhymes, to show different numbers, making numbers in different ways or increasing, decreasing and doubles patterns. Some rhymes use larger numbers, like 'Ten in the bed'. Most can easily be extended: for instance, with 'Five little ducks' you can start with ten ducks and adapt to two ducks swimming away each day. A rhyme like 'Five currant buns in the baker's shop', where children come in turn and pay a penny for the buns, demonstrates exchanging one penny for one bun and can be illustrated with props including numerals. This demonstrates the 'one less than' pattern with the decreasing buns and the 'one more than' pattern with increasing pennies. A magnet board and tape recorder makes this an independent activity for children to rehearse the language and actions involved, so they can explore the pattern. This could also be shown on an interactive whiteboard. Rhyme cards can be stored in bags with their respective props, such as soft toys or magnetic pictures.

Some stories also contain number patterns and can be used in a similar way to rhymes, with the advantage that pictures can be copied and used as props, and some have matching puppets available (see, for example, Carle 1974; Inkpen 1993). A few stories have number as a main theme (see, for example, Hutchins 1986; Inkpen 1998). Rather than ruin good stories by making children count the things on the page, you can tell your own simple number stories (as in Chapter 6). A box or basket with props in it for storytelling can become a daily feature. Asking children to shut their eyes and imagine helps them to visualise: 'You go to the park and see a dog and four squirrels. The dog chases the squirrels and one runs up a tree, then one hides in the waste paper bin. How many can you see?' Encouraging children to use their fingers helps them keep track.

Other group time activities can involve:

- puppets with number problems or difficulties in counting
- a washing line with mixed up numbers, or bags with different numbers of things
- puzzles and problems, such as 'Guess how many's in the jar?'

These activities involve rehearsal of numbers and numerals, spotting patterns and errors, communicating, predicting and problem solving.

Number games

As discussed previously, games which involve filling spaces with counters are more accessible for younger children, so they can count movable objects. Counting 'moves' along a track is much harder: young children tend to count the spaces instead, including the one they are on, so they are always one short of the moves they should have made. Children can use beans, pennies, little plastic animals or toys, according to current interests. They can fill up a baseboard each, using their own dice and play independently or take turns with a friend. This sort of game can provide a lot of assessment information. For instance, do the children:

- subitise the dots on the dice?
- count out a number from a larger group?
- count to check the number of things?
- correct a miscount by adding or subtracting?

Children can also discuss who has more and how many they have altogether. Long tracks will involve big numbers. A numeral dice will help children relate numerals to amounts and may include zero and numbers to ten. (For examples, see BEAM Education 2002.)

Games involving skill, such as skittles, can involve children in scoring by finding a numeral, keying in the score on a calculator or recording in their own way. Games include basketball, throwing beanbags in crates or tyres, or throwing hoops over canes. Playing skittles involves counting those knocked down and also those still standing, demonstrating subtraction and number bonds. Children can be challenged to throw five things, so that number bonds for five and the language of 'How many more?' are rehearsed.

Number challenges can emerge from other activities which involve skill, such as catching magnetic fish or picking up peas with chopsticks or seeds with tweezers. 'How many things can you fit in?' is a popular activity with small containers like film canisters or teaspoons, together with pennies, beans or jewels.

A nursery nurse invented an activity with interlocking plastic shapes, where children made different shaped 'houses' for little plastic bears and predicted how many they would be able to fit in. When they found out, they challenged other children to guess and some wrote the number on post-its. This was engaging because it was practically creative and surprisingly hard to predict how many bears would fit in the 'houses' of different shapes and sizes.

Children can devise their own games from a selection of apparatus such as tracks, dice and counters. With an outdoor number track, children can throw a beanbag on to a number and then jump to it, or throw a giant dice and do that many jumps. Indoors, covering up numbers on a track with blank tiles, then throwing a dice, poses the challenge of uncovering the matching number: this can involve a floor number track and giant dice or a table top version. Numbered 'stepping stones' can provide a range of challenges, as described in Chapter 7. A popular game in one nursery involved children throwing a giant dice then jumping on that many giant shapes on the floor. Number games and activities like these therefore involve children rehearsing skills, but also predicting and problem solving, making connections between the different uses for numbers, communicating and correcting each other.

How many ways?

Exploring different visual arrangements of numbers of objects helps children to gain cardinal meanings for the numbers. It is also an investigative activity which allows children choice, control and the opportunity to spot patterns. 'Show me four' using fingers is one way of doing this. Five year olds can make lots of different arrangements for the same number, using counters, 'matchsticks' or cubes (Baratta-Lorton 1976). Putting these on individual pieces of card with the written number helps children focus. They can also explore different number patterns by sticking, printing or stamping shapes. Children can talk about the numbers they can see within their arrangement, for instance describing patterns for six as 'three and three', 'two and two and two' or 'one and two and three'. This helps them see small numbers making up bigger numbers and to become aware of part-whole relationships. Number experts can then go on to partition numbers, for instance making their own dominoes or number bond patterns (see Fig. 8.8). These kinds of activities invite children to discover their own patterns and to talk about them.

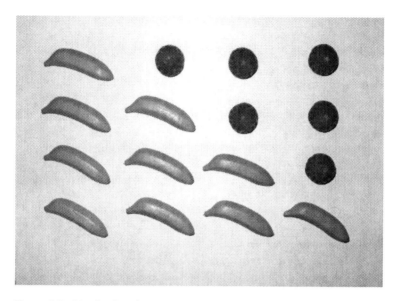

Figure 8.8   Number bond patterns with bananas and strawberries

Number hunt

'We're going on a number hunt! We're not scared! We're not scared!'
An exciting outdoors activity for rehearsing number recognition is to
hide some numerals in the garden and send children off to see how
many they can find. In one nursery, they chanted a version of *We're
Going on a Bear Hunt* (Rosen 2001). The children rushed off, came back
with numbers and pegged them on the washing line. Adults challenged children to find particular numbers: 'Kavita's hunting for
number seven!'

Numeral cards can have the number of dots on them, or children
can be challenged to find pairs of matching numeral and dot cards. A
reception class teacher challenged the class to stand with their numbers in order before the sand-timer ran out, creating great excitement.
To encourage counting, one reception teacher hid a different number
of things in the classroom each day, so the children had to find ten
dinosaurs one day and 15 elephants the next. This provided addition
and subtraction problems, as the children knew the total and some

could work out how many more there were to find. A variation is to hide a lot of objects in the sand and for the children to see how many they can find. For instance, sieving sequins on to plates encourages counting to high numbers. Number hunts encourage rehearsal of number recognition as well as the development of very positive attitudes to numbers.

ICT

Fuson (1988) suggested that many children in the USA learned to count and recognise numbers from *Sesame Street*. In the UK, the BBC 'Number Time' jingle helped many children to remember the number sequence. In providing multisensory and musical stimulus, ICT is a valuable resource, although some practitioners might say children spend enough time watching videos at home. Many interactive programmes require children to match pictures and numerals and provide feedback. Digital cameras can also provide pictures of numerals in the local environment. Programmable robots give children an understanding that greater numbers make them go further. ICT activities usually provide rehearsal and problem solving experiences: with adult assistance, they encourage reflection on strategies.

9 Shape and space

During the Froebel Blockplay Project (Gura 1992: 53) some children learned to build towers as tall as they could reach: so the staff introduced stepstools to help them build even higher. Gura reports that soon after this, four year old Seema announced that she was going to build a tall tower. She mounted the steps, hesitated and then asked, 'Can you start up here?' When an adult handed her a block, she said, 'You can't. You can't start up here.'

One of the problems with early learning about shape and space is that adults cannot remember not knowing such things, making it hard to identify the learning in activities like blockplay. Seema presumably visualised building a tower from the top down. This is spatial thinking, which some mathematicians would argue is one of the most important and underrated kinds of mathematical thinking.

What is 'shape and space'?

Learning aims for geometry, or 'shape and space' as it is usually referred to in the primary years, can seem elusive at an early level. Practitioners and parents may not be clear about its importance compared to number learning. Pre-school geometry can become reduced to 'barking at shapes', where the main aim is for children to name squares, circles or triangles. The 'space' aspect may also be seen as just using positional vocabulary. Official curricula like the Early Learning Goals (DfEE/QCA 2000) may be responsible for this, with their emphasis on vocabulary. Some goals, like 'Use developing mathematical ideas and methods to solve practical problems,' encourage more creative activity, like Seema's self-set problem of building a very tall tower. However, it is not clear what 'mathematical ideas' about shape and space young children should understand. Educators need to know how children learn shape and space concepts in order to support learning and to decide what strategies to use. With Seema, silently handing over the block was all that was required to prompt her thinking: effective teaching may involve subtle strategies. The Blockplay Project did not set children challenges or provide direction. Instead, the approach was to make provision, encourage and talk to children, while recording what went on, with notable results. Effective teaching included all that had gone before in the classroom to foster Seema's enthusiasm and confidence, including the provision of the blocks and the steps.

So what mathematics of 'shape and space' is accessible and important for three to fives to learn? Usually 'shape' at lower primary level focuses on classifying shapes according to their properties, whereas 'space' includes classifying positions, direction and movement (see DfEE/QCA 1999).

Shape

Shape usually involves recognising similarities and differences between properties. With two and three dimensional shapes, there are four basic kinds of shape properties with associated vocabulary, some of which, like parallelism, young children may recognise intuitively but not name:

- 'curvedness'
    curved or straight (2D shapes)
    curved, round or flat (3D shapes)
- numbers
    of corners and sides (2D)
    of vertices, edges and faces (3D)
- length of sides
    equal or not
    parallel or not
- size of angles
    right angles
    larger or smaller than a right angle (obtuse or acute)

- for 3D shapes, knowing the 2D shapes of their faces.

The names of shapes usually included for the early years are:

- circle, square, triangle and rectangle (2D)
- cube, cuboid (box shape), cone, sphere (3D).

In order to sort shapes mathematically, children must first understand their properties. To distinguish triangles from non-triangles (such as pizza slices) children must recognise three corners and distinguish straight from curved sides. This implies that the language of properties is as important as shape names and that understanding is as important as the vocabulary.

Pattern is often associated with shape and space. Mathematically, pattern means more than making visual arrangements. It involves recognising rules and relationships, such as that two right angled shapes can always fit together to make a straight edge. This suggests that there is more to learning about shapes than sorting them. Fielker (1973) argued that children should be doing mathematics by investigating the way shapes behave and the relationships between properties. As with number, primary geometry could involve operations such as combining and taking shapes apart in different ways. If children discover that two triangles can make a square, they are recognising equivalence with shapes (Coltman *et al.* 2002). This view emphasises the importance of creative, exploratory activities like blockplay and making pictures and patterns with shapes.

Visualising spatially is also emphasised by Fielker. This is defined by Clements (2004), in a summary of research on geometric and spatial thinking, as 'the ability to generate and manipulate images'. For instance, a child intending to make a box might visualise what shapes are needed for the faces. Fielker (1993) calls this 'mental geometry', arguing that it should have the same status as mental arithmetic. Anghileri and Baron (1999) found that children were better able to solve problems with 3D shapes if they could visualise turning and combining them in different ways.

Space

Space is a more complex area of learning to define. It includes:

- positions and directions, such as inside/outside, on top of/ underneath, in front/behind, left/right
- movement and transformations, such as:
    translating – sliding images sideways, up and down, or diagonally
    reflecting – 'flipping' or reversing images
    rotating – turning images.

Young children begin to represent spatial relations in drawings, models and maps. They learn that a jigsaw piece might be made to fit by sliding, flipping or turning. Printing and tiling patterns on fabrics or buildings in many cultures have used transformations: nowadays children can produce these using computer programs. Children can begin to visualise how things appear from a different viewpoint or to imagine turning a square or repeating a pattern. The early shape and space curriculum therefore links with areas such as geography and art.

What is the importance of learning about shape and space?

Arithmetic has traditionally been seen as more important than geometry (see, for instance, Thumpston 1994). Perhaps this is because adults had a surfeit of Euclidean proofs, which are not as obviously useful in everyday life (although the 3, 4, 5 triangle has been useful for creating right angles in buildings since the Egyptian pyramids (Hopkins *et al.* 2004).

The Royal Society (2001) identified reasons for teaching geometry at secondary level, several of which also apply to the early years. They include:

- to develop an awareness of the historical and cultural heritage of geometry in society
- to develop spatial awareness, geometrical intuition and the ability to visualise
- to engender a positive attitude to mathematics.

Geometry is important to art, design and architecture in all cultures. Jones and Mooney (2003) pointed out that many recent technological developments in design, construction and science depend on geometric modelling, including robotics, brain scanning, global positioning systems and computer animation. Visualising is obviously a key skill for such innovations. Some people have greater strengths with spatial thinking than arithmetic and some high achievers in maths, particularly males, are stronger spatially than verbally (Friedman 1995). The ability to rotate shapes mentally (an important aspect of spatial visualising) is greater in males. This is associated with greater success with word problems, suggesting that spatial thinking might help in visualising mathematical problems (Delgado and Prieto 2004). As discussed previously, young children begin by thinking spatially: it therefore makes sense to build on this to develop positive attitudes to mathematical learning.

How do children learn about shape and space?

Analysis of children's learning about shape and space has been influenced by Piagetian theory, which emphasised young children constructing mental representations through reflection on action. Through experience, children learn about the permanency of objects which roll out of sight: they can visualise the toy behind the sofa and routes to retrieve it. Piaget argued that young children could not recognise projective and Euclidean properties. Projective properties include positional relations which change according to the viewpoint and also straight or curved lines. According to the Piagetian view, the egocentric young child was unable to predict how things would appear from different viewpoints. Euclidean properties include size, angle and numbers of sides and corners. Piagetian theory held that children's development followed the logical structure of mathematics, so they understood topological properties first (Piaget and Inhelder 1956). (Topology includes properties like whether shapes are open or closed, or made up of connected regions like a figure 8. A square, triangle and circle are topologically equivalent, because they are all simple closed shapes, which can be made from a single line: hence topology is sometimes called 'rubber geometry'.) This view has since been discredited by research: babies can tell squares from circles and three year olds can predict what others can see from a different viewpoint (Dickson *et al.* 1984). Thorpe (1995) claimed that younger children explored topological properties before Euclidean ones, in that children played with the positions of objects before sorting shapes, but this is not topology in the mathematical sense, according to Dickson *et al.* They suggested that young children failed at the Piagetian tasks because they were simply too complex.

Schema

Schema are spatial movement patterns which have been observed in babies and young children, following Piagetian theory (Athey 1990). For instance, children may repeat actions, like up and down, or circling, and use similar forms when arranging objects, or in drawing, persisting with the same action schema for some time. Gura (1992) suggested that children's schema might be related to the acquisition of construction techniques, such as making towers or enclosures. Athey and others suggested identifying and supporting children's schema, by providing related resources and experiences such as things which rotate or enveloping activities. Nutbrown (1999) argued that this approach helped children understand advanced spatial concepts such as tessellation and area. However, Davis and Pepper (1992) described children sharing biscuits as using a 'dealing' schema, an automatic activity not involving reflection. It is difficult to assess whether children are learning spatial concepts when apparently engaged in a schema. For instance, a child who suggested putting the new baby's cot in a cupboard in a cave was identified as following an enveloping schema. Athey argued this interpretation gave a more positive view of children's behaviour. While this may be true, focusing on the spatial behaviour and ignoring its social significance seems to ignore Vygotskian views on learning.

Children's drawings have been interpreted as revealing geometrical understanding. Athey found Piaget's 'topological' progression in children's drawings and representations. However, there are alternative theories influencing interpretations of children's drawings: some suggest there are innate preferences for certain forms, especially symmetrical ones. Goodnow (1977) found that children went to great lengths to avoid drawing people with hair crossing over their arms. Young children's reluctance to draw things as overlapping has been interpreted as a lack of awareness of perspective, but it may reflect a stylistic choice. Anning (2002) found that early years practitioners were reluctant to 'tune into' children's meanings in their drawings, especially those relating to current culture, such as fashion or cars, preferring to focus on forms. Caution therefore needs to be exercised in interpreting children's spatial behaviour and representations as indicating mathematical learning. However, it seems that young children periodically focus on certain spatial movements and forms, which adults could encourage them to talk and think about.

Progression in learning about shape

Teacher: How do you know it's a triangle?
Child: Because it's got three shapes!

Children can recognise geometric shapes from an early age: two year olds can 'post' a shape in its matching hole and three year olds can name shapes. According to Clements (2004), drawing shapes is more problematic. Whereas four year olds may spontaneously draw triangles, they have difficulty copying them. Recognising irregular examples of shapes is even more difficult. Clements *et al.* (1999) found that six year olds could not identify irregular examples of triangles. They rejected asymmetrical examples 'because the point on top is not in the middle', and also ones that were 'too pointy' or 'too flat', preferring those with the same height as width. Children also did not recognise rectangles which were 'too skinny' or 'not wide enough'; they preferred those with length twice the height. Children had difficulty distinguishing non-examples of shapes: they wrongly identified parallelograms as rectangles. Young children therefore seemed to recognise geometrical shapes by matching them to an ideal image or prototype.

People from cultures which are not familiar with geometric shapes tended to select regular ones as 'best examples', suggesting that we may have a hard-wired preference for closed, symmetrical shapes, according to Clements. As most apparatus and books tend to present limited examples of shapes, Clements argued that educational settings reinforced misconceptions, rather than extending children's shape concepts.

Mathematical shape classification depends on definitions: a triangle is any closed 2D shape with three straight sides and three corners. Therefore, a slice of pizza is not a triangle because it has a curved side and a musical triangle is not a mathematical triangle because it has a gap in it. 'Nearly but not quite' examples like these can help to clarify what defines a shape. Some children may also confuse names for 2D and 3D shapes, calling a pyramid a triangle. (Technically, of course, any example of a triangle made out of plastic, wood or paper, no matter how thin, is a solid shape because it has a thickness and only the faces are triangles.) Providing a variety of examples can help children to identify common properties.

The orientation of shapes is also an issue: some children reject examples which do not have a horizontal base, like the nine year old who said an equilateral triangle with a vertical side was not a triangle 'because it fell over' (Dickson *et al*. 1984). Clements reported that primary age children commonly assert that a turned square was 'not a square any more, it's a diamond'. Computer programs can provide experience of turning shapes so they are seen in different orientations. For pre-school children, examples of shapes should also vary in colour and material: one child said that a shape was a triangle 'because it's blue', probably because all triangles were blue in the nursery's set of shapes. The same child might also believe that geometric shapes were always made of plastic.

Recognising shapes

'Recognising shapes' therefore involves more than just matching or naming them. Children can only be said to understand the concepts of geometric shapes when they can identify a variety of examples in different orientations and discriminate between examples and non-examples. Being able to explain why a shape is not a triangle is a more valid assessment than naming an equilateral triangle with a horizontal base. This may be beyond most pre-school children. Dickson *et al*. recommended van Hiele's (1986) progression of children's shape concepts as a guide to curriculum provision:

- level 1: holistic shape recognition
- level 2: awareness of properties, for instance through constructing shapes
- level 3: beginning to reason according to definitions.

Clements *et al*. (1999: 206) gave examples of holistic, visual responses such as children saying a shape was a rectangle, because it 'just looked like one' or because 'it looks like a door'. They argued that there was also a pre-recognition level 0, when children did not reliably distinguish between examples and non-examples. They also found that when children recognised shapes consistently, they combined reasoning with reliance on prototypes, synthesising visual and analytical thinking. Whereas van Hiele proposed that level 3 was not reached until the later primary years, Clements *et al.* suggested that levels of thinking co-existed, dependent on children's experience rather than age-linked development. Similarly, Coltman *et al.* (2002) found that children operated at different levels with different shapes. They could predict which way round to turn a cuboid to match a 2D shape, but did not try to turn a triangular prism. This suggests that children's familiarity with shapes affects their thinking. Coltman *et al.* also found that scaffolding children's problem solving, for instance by encouraging them to look harder at shape faces, had marked effects on their use of shape knowledge.

Children's constructions can show awareness of properties: Imran's fairground wheel in Fig. 9.1 has equal lengths for the radii of the circle, with shorter blocks substituted when he ran out of long blocks. The teddy's bed (see Chapter 10, Fig. 10.1) shows a rectangle

Figure 9.1 Imran's fairground wheel

constructed with right angles and opposite sides equal. The nursery child who said the triangle had 'three shapes' showed reasoning based on some awareness of the threeness of triangles. It is not clear how competent young children are at this kind of reasoning because, as Clements argues, they may be limited by the examples they have met. It therefore seems that children's learning about shape concepts develops in a complex way, involving experience, visualising and reasoning, supported by teaching.

Language

The language initially used by young children to describe shapes may not be mathematical. They tend to use informal words like 'pointy' or 'slanty', or analogies like 'house shaped' or 'ball'. Clements *et al.* (1999) found that many five year olds referred to a circle as 'round'. Informal language can show that children are attending to concepts like 'angle' or 'sphere', but it may also limit the ways in which children think about shapes. Coltman *et al.* (2002) suggested that children who called a triangular prism a 'roof' shape were less likely to turn it 'upright'. Adults providing mathematical language helped children to think more analytically and to connect their actions with results. Making comments like 'It's not falling down now you've used flat surfaces' helps a child identify which properties have made the tower more stable.

Classifying shapes

The mathematical system of classifying shapes is quite complex, with categories forming subsets of each other. The set of quadrilaterals (four sided shapes) includes parallelograms, with opposite sides equal. Rectangles are a subset of parallelograms with right angles, and squares are special rectangles, with all sides equal. Rectangles can therefore be very long and thin or almost square, and also exactly square (see Fig. 9.2).

This comes as a surprise to adults who were not taught mathematical definitions for shapes, but think instead of a visual image with two long sides and two short sides. Young children can understand there are special cases with particular names: for instance, they may learn that kittens are a special kind of cat. Clements found that five year olds invented the term 'square rectangles' in the context of a

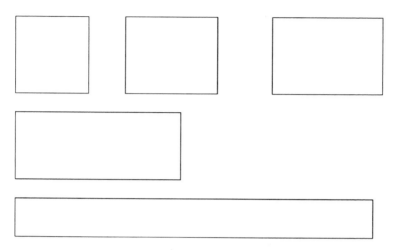

Figure 9.2 A continuum of rectangles

computer program. Elia and Gagatsis (2003) introduced four to seven year olds to a range of rectangles by systematically varying the sides so that they became more equal. They found that children understood that squares were at one end of a continuum of rectangle shapes. This suggests that computer experience may help develop children's understanding of shapes, enabling them to investigate a greater variety of examples. If children call a square 'a rectangle', adults are faced with a dilemma. To say they are wrong would be misleading and 'intellectually dishonest', as Elia and Gagatsis argued. Calling it a 'special' or 'square rectangle' seems the most appropriate response, even if unfamiliar to the adults involved. Some teachers avoid the problem by referring to 'oblongs': these are non-square rectangles. However, referring to non-characteristics is not in keeping with the inclusive system of classification and merely postpones the introduction of the word 'rectangle', which children may know already.

In summary, it is more important to focus on young children's awareness of shape properties rather than shape labelling and to develop this through providing opportunities to discriminate, discuss and play with a variety of examples in a range of contexts and with a range of materials, including ICT.

Angles

The concept of angles is generally considered to develop later and is related to the idea of direction. Sarama (2004) found that five year olds did not pay attention to angles when matching or fitting shapes. Much older children have misconceptions with angles, believing, for instance, that they are determined by the length of lines (Dickson *et al.*, 1984). The recognition of right angles may have an intuitive aspect: Goodnow (1977) found children preferred them in drawings, but identifying them precisely is more difficult. However, young children may discriminate between angles and refer to obtuse triangles as 'fat' and acute triangles as 'pointy'. Children who fit four squares round a point, or put six triangles together to make a hexagon, may be selecting and learning about angles. Five year olds using robots or LOGO microworlds readily learn how to create a right angle turn: experience of angle as movement may heighten children's awareness. It is recommended that children learn about angle as a measurement of turn (DfEE/QCA 1999). Exploring properties of shape through movement, such as walking round shapes or making body shapes, seems potentially helpful for visualising angles.

Children's construction

Children's construction demonstrates mathematical progression, according to research. The Blockplay Project (Gura 1992) found that individuals varied in preferring abstract or representational constructions and that their development depended on acquiring a repertoire of building techniques. Younger children, according to Anghileri and Baron (1999), chose randomly from shapes, attempted to build on slopes and points and were surprised when structures fell. Older children made compound shapes, towers and used symmetry. Older children's blockplay was also more 'detailed and structurally integrated', with greater concern for visual harmony. The Blockplay Project found progression which confirmed previous research, from linear to three dimensional and from simple to complex:

- linear – vertical towers and horizontal lines
- 2D – filling in or covering an area; enclosures (e.g. beds and fields) and arches
- 3D – solids; hollow (e.g. boats, houses with rooms).

Even with the expert five year olds, truly three dimensional constructions were rare, and most were intended to be seen from one viewpoint only: 3D enclosures complete with 'roof' require considerable expertise.

A further stage might be children's ability to draw their constructions, which some could do as accurately as the adults, showing sizes and numbers of blocks (see Fig. 9.3). One child drew her caterpillar (seen in Fig. 9.5, p. 126) and later got out her drawing in order to remake it and corrected the number of legs shown, demonstrating an ability to interpret a diagram. Some children may be familiar with

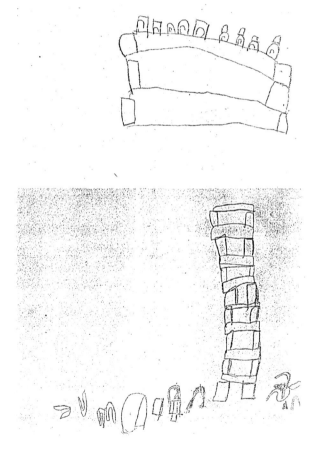

Figure 9.3 Children's drawings of their constructions

building models from pictures in construction kits. Dijk *et al.* (2004) noted that children usually refused when asked to draw their models, unless there was a clear communicative purpose, such as to provide instructions for younger children.

Clements (2004) proposed a progression in combining shapes to make units, identifying children as:

- precomposers – using one shape to stand for one object, for example a block as a mobile phone
- piece assemblers – using one shape as a part of an object, for example a block as a table leg
- picture makers – using several shapes for one item, for example several blocks for a leg
- shape composers – showing intentionality, for example selecting blocks, then making a window
- substitution composers – deliberately making units out of other shapes, for example making a succession of arches with three blocks at a time, using two triangles to make a square.

Beyond this stage, children make units which are made up of other units, for instance making patterns of squares made up of triangles.

The identification of progressions does not imply that children should be directed along such lines. As the Blockplay Project found, giving status to children's constructions, with adults discussing, drawing and photographing them, was the most effective teaching strategy. Lines of development depend on children's experience and interests, as well as maturity. However, different ways of analysing and evaluating compositions can help adults to appreciate children's learning. Construction, supported by adults, is likely to help children's spatial knowledge, by giving them experience of how things fit together in three dimensions and encouraging them to plan, visualise and reason.

Progression in learning about space

Visualising spatial positions in 3D is particularly challenging for young children. Gura (1992: 31) recounted that some five and six year olds froze when they heard a noise in the room above them. They were told it was just people moving furniture. ' "What, on the ceiling?" was one incredulous response'. Even when taken to see the room, the children seemed to have difficulty understanding that 'one man's ceiling is another man's floor'.

Spatial orientation

Spatial orientation is identified by various writers as an important dimension of spatial thinking. It is sometimes distinguished from spatial visualisation, involving changing positions rather than shapes. However, definitions vary: Friedman (1995) identified orientation as spatial reasoning, including the ability to mentally rotate shapes. Clements called spatial orientation 'knowing the shape of one's environment', which he argued was a cognitive strength for young children. This includes ideas of:

- position or location – 'knowing where you are'
- direction or navigation – 'knowing how to get around'.

Clements emphasised young children's spatial understanding as being firstly in relation to themselves, reflecting Piagetian theory. 'Location' includes being able to identify positions, predicting what things will look like from different points of view and being able to understand and represent viewpoints as shown with models, maps or plans. The ability to mentally rotate shapes, to understand different viewpoints and to represent shapes using perspective is therefore connected to understanding position and location. Dickson *et al.* (1984) suggest that consistent positions such as above and below are easier to understand than left and right, which are relative to the viewer and change according to the viewpoint. This suggests two levels of difficulty for positions and directions:

- fixed – for example, inside/outside; between; on top of/ below; over/under
- relative – for example, in front/behind; forwards/backwards; left/right.

Children also find positions harder to identify when the objects are small and further away from a reference point such as themselves or a wall. In making maps of classrooms, children tend to position things near the walls more correctly than objects grouped in the middle of the room (Liben and Yekel 1996).

Navigation, according to Clements, includes visualising routes and predicting what you should see next. This helps in checking that you are on the right route and in deciding which direction to take next, which is obviously an important life skill. Two year old Tom, on the way to a familiar holiday venue, suddenly said 'Horses next!' before the car turned the bend and horses could be seen in the field. Tom's prediction was presumably based on his memory of a sequence of landmarks, which Clements suggests is a first step for children. Piaget *et al.* (1960) also identified that very young children could identify directions, for instance pointing to where home was. Clements outlined a development in children's navigational understanding, which is similar to that of Piaget:

- landmarks: three year olds can make meaningful maps with 'landscape toys' such as houses, cars and trees
- routes: children then make connected sequences of landmarks
- scaled routes: older children show relative distances between landmarks for familiar paths
- mental maps: routes and locations are combined.

Clements also summarised research about map learning for three and four year olds and older children. Understanding maps includes ideas of direction, distance and location; symbols on maps may also require an understanding of perspective, as with squares used for houses.

Three year olds can demonstrate understanding non-verbally. They can:

- represent their environment with real size objects – for instance, arranging classroom furniture to match their own classroom
- demonstrate the route from their seat to the teacher's desk by walking
- group toy houses and cars in terms of rough proximity, but not in correct position to each other.

Four year olds can:

- learn a route from a map – children who were shown a plan first were better at finding their way through a series of

rooms, compared with children who had only navigated the route
- reconstruct a room from a plan
- use simple co-ordinates and identify the intersection of two sightlines.

However, only older children can:

- interpret where they are on the map
- align a map to face the way they are looking
- draw maps
- represent distances
- recognise features on aerial photos and area maps.

Clements emphasises that there is a maturational element in following maps which requires a large mental processing capacity to update directions and locations (although children can be taught to consciously check maps as they go). Liben and Yekel (1996) found four and five year old children had difficulty positioning items on a plan of their classroom. Giving them experience of a raised view from a chair on a scaffold did not help them. However, an oblique map, where the tables were shown with legs, did help, because it gave them pictorial clues to the objects shown. It seems that young children have difficulty with the symbolic nature of maps: children shown a map with tennis courts thought these were doors and also expected red roads to be red in reality. Children occasionally draw a plan view of constructions, when standing with a clipboard looking down (see Chapter 11, Fig. 11.2). Young children's drawings often use a mixture of perspectives, as with Marie's elephant (Fig 9.5, p. 126) which shows the side view, except for the head, which is plan view, showing both tusks.

Children's navigational skills are improved by giving each other directions to follow a route, presumably because articulating these helps them to focus and remember. According to Clements, activities involving ICT also help: walking a path then directing a robot or representing it on a computer helps develop visualisation. There are various maze programs which help children to tell left from right. Teaching children to make maps of their own area and to recognise symbols on maps also improves their understanding. Developing children's understanding of location and navigation therefore is an important aspect of developing their spatial orientation.

Transformations

The ability to describe movements mathematically begins with children understanding directions like left and right, forwards and backwards. Turning involves ideas of angle, as discussed previously. Children can investigate transformations, or the effects of movements like turning, sliding or flipping, in a variety of activities, like jigsaw puzzles, printing or using mirrors. Computer programs and robots are useful for providing feedback about predictions.

The following progression, suggested by Piagetian theory, has been confirmed by research (Dickson *et al.* 1984). Children find recognising transformations easier than constructing them, which requires them to visualise. They also find transforming shapes in some directions easier than others:

- Translation (sliding) is easier horizontally or vertically, and harder diagonally. This transformation is common on printed fabric, wallpaper and wrapping paper and in patterns and designs from many cultures.
- Reflection (flipping) is easier horizontally than vertically: young children can reflect a pattern sideways, but not from top to bottom. Again, oblique reflections, across a diagonal line, are more difficult. Children use reflective symmetry intuitively in their own constructions and patterns. However, sometimes an impression of mirror symmetry is achieved accidentally by simply repeating units, without any reversal involved, as in the pattern in Fig 9.4.
- Rotation (turning) is more difficult, especially predicting what shapes will look like when turned round, as Anghileri and Baron (1999) found. However, young children use rotation when solving jigsaw puzzles. Sarama (2004: 374) developed materials in the USA with five to seven year olds working practically with 'pattern block' shapes and then with matching computer programs including a 'shape puzzle', which had 'slide' and 'turn' tools to help children fill a frame with shapes. She found that even the youngest children used rotation as much as reflection to make the shapes fit. She concluded that 'pre-schoolers

Figure 9.4   A pattern with repeated units

can do more than we assume, especially working with computers'.

- More difficult transformations include enlargement (making smaller or larger). Clements noted that children could identify similarity or enlargements when working with computers.

It therefore seems likely that mathematical activities which build on children's interests and encourage them to investigate and solve puzzles by moving shapes in different ways, develop their spatial visualisation skills. Children hear movement language in stories and use it when describing their own movements or those of figures in small world play. They can follow instructions and instruct each other, then instruct robots, such as Roamer and Pixie, or figures in computer games. Increased exposure to this kind of activity seems likely to increase children's facility at an early age.

How cognitive learning processes relate to shape and space

The learning processes previously identified are equally applicable to shape and space: they also suggest a range of appropriate teaching strategies.

Learning through observation, instruction and rehearsal

Children in the Froebel projects reported (Athey 1990; Gura 1992) made progress partly due to the sheer amount of experience in representing and constructing. Gura reported that children who had not had experience with the blocks for some time had to go back and revise some previous stages before they could regain their expertise. Rehearsal in shape and space might include using mathematical vocabulary and practising schemas, building or drawing techniques and spatial patterns.

Making connections and generalising

Making connections implies understanding the way shapes behave in space: it involves sorting shapes and making patterns. For instance, children may notice properties of curved and flat shapes, that curved solids roll easily and flat shapes stack. They learn which shapes can be made out of other shapes or that four blocks fit together around a point (underpinning the idea that four right angles make 360 degrees). With spatial relations children learn, for instance, that reflection involves reversing the order of things: AB becomes BA. If teachers identify what relationships children might spot, they can provide resources and intervene appropriately.

Representing, talking and symbolising

Children's representations can demonstrate their discrimination of shape properties. Marie's elephant (see Fig. 9.5) used circles for eyes and cylinders for legs, suggesting that she noticed the resemblance between these shape properties in the elephant and the blocks. She selected the elliptical curve for the trunk and the quarter circles for the elephant's rump, showing that she not only could discriminate straight from curved, but also could identify different kinds of curves. Marie also chose to combine side and overhead viewpoints, by showing both tusks.

Trying to make figurative models and pictures involves children in creative solutions, for instance in finding shapes with the same properties as those they want to represent. Talking about what they are doing in their own words, with adults providing commentaries and vocabulary, is important in helping children become aware of spatial relationships. Giving instructions helps children learn about directions. What children try to represent seems immaterial: for instance, animals stimulate geometrical drawings and block constructions. Spatial representation can involve a variety of media,

Figure 9.5   Marie's elephant

including clay, recycled materials, structured resources and toys, paint or pencil, and also gesture, whole body shapes and movement. Another important aspect is the visualisation of shapes and positions.

Predicting prior to feedback

Trying to predict develops visualisation and many shape and space activities provide intrinsic feedback. For instance, design problems, like trying to make a bed for a teddy, involve trial and adjustment, and children can make many predictions while adjusting the components until it looks right. Puzzles and computer programs, where shapes have to be chosen to match, or turned to fit, also encourage prediction and give feedback. Giving instructions to make a robot follow a route encourages prediction with directions. More structured activities focus children's attention: for instance, copying a design requires closer attention to shape and positions than creating one from the imagination. Adult-led activities like guessing the shape in the feely bag also encourage prediction and reasoning.

Spotting errors, incongruity and misconceptions

Providing non-examples of shapes, like triangles with a corner slightly cut off, or 'tricky' examples, like skewed triangles, are effective teaching strategies for clarifying misconceptions. As with number activities, a puppet can be used to make mistakes, such as giving wrong directions or descriptions.

Metacognition or reflecting on thinking

Encouraging children to explain how shapes have been sorted or why they have been chosen for a model can help them become aware of their thinking. Problem solving and designing involves children in reflecting, checking their progress and refining solutions. Adults can support this by modelling decision making and evaluation processes.

Teaching approaches

The two Froebel projects reported considerable progress in the children's learning, suggesting some effective teaching principles (Athey 1990; Gura 1992). Provision of stimulating resources was key: in Athey's project, visits provided children with a desire to represent what they had seen. With blockplay, one parent was heard to remark of her child's impressively complex construction, 'She never does anything like this at home.' This did not seem surprising, since the child had been given sole use of several hundred pounds worth of unit blocks. Similarly, the pattern in Fig. 9.6 was only created because the school had acquired a lot of these particular shapes, without which this creation would have been impossible. Quality provision therefore contributes to quality learning. Secondly, the adults listened and talked to the children, encouraging them to articulate their thinking. Thirdly, and perhaps most importantly, the projects gave status to the children's learning. Adults recorded the children's representations and comments, took photos and drew their constructions, reported them, analysed them and discussed them with parents, all of which must have raised children's self-esteem. This underlines

Figure 9.6 A pattern with arch blocks

the social and emotional dimensions of learning about shape and space.

Activities

Considering how children learn indicates that both open-ended and structured resources and activities are needed. A rich variety of shapes, construction material, fabrics, environmental artefacts and visits allow connections to be made and patterns spotted. These can draw on children's cultural heritage. Structured resources and focused activities, including puzzles, games, problems, stories and design projects, computer programs and robots, will also encourage children to visualise and articulate their thinking. Some of these resources will stimulate learning of both shape and space, whereas others focus attention more on one aspect than the other. The following list summarises the main opportunities for shape and space learning and identifies the main mathematical ideas and learning processes involved.

Shape and space

Making figurative or abstract constructions, pictures and patterns, 3D or 2D
Selecting shapes to make models, representing shape properties
For example, making pictures of a farm visit on an interactive whiteboard

Following examples or diagrams to make models or patterns
Identifying and selecting exact shapes and positions
For example, copying a pattern or design from a photo of a child's work

Describing shape properties and spatial relations in play, stories and experiences
Using positional and shape language
For example, retelling a story about a journey with props

Collaboratively rearranging play areas and discussing options
Selecting shapes to fit, changing positions, using positional and shape language

For example, setting up a role-play area, laying a table for a party, making a den outdoors

PE and dance activities: making shapes with their bodies or movements, walking shape outlines
Making straight and curved movements and shapes, turning and rotating in different directions
For example, fireworks dancing

Designing with landscape toys, drawing maps of imaginary and familiar places, and using maps
Selecting shapes to use, representing and describing positions and directions
For example, making a map to get to the headteacher's room

Folding and unfolding, making paper cut-outs
Visualising and identifying properties like reflective symmetry or relationships between shapes, like two triangles make a square
For example, predicting what shape a table cloth will be when unfolded

Shape and pattern in the environment, on surfaces, objects, buildings, materials, fabric, taking photos, displaying artefacts and identifying shapes and patterns
Describing shapes, properties and transformations, using shape and space vocabulary
For example, photo display of children's shoe sole patterns, with speech bubbles

Using light effects, such as overhead projectors, light boxes, torches, shadows, mirrors and reflections
Describing shape properties, changes and positions
For example, making arrangements with objects, letters or shapes on a light box

Focusing on shape properties

Sorting shapes, finding ones that match, odd ones out
Recognising properties like the number of sides, straight or curved

For example, sorting 'triangles and not triangles' from a collection, including irregular triangles of different colours and sizes, and non-examples such as a 'triangle' musical instrument, a triangle with a corner cut off, a pizza slice, a pyramid

Hidden shapes
Visualising shapes, reasoning about shape properties
For example:

- **screened shapes**: show a bit of a shape with the rest hidden behind a screen – for example, show one corner of a triangle and ask, 'What might it be?' 'What could it not be?' 'Why?'
- **feely bag**: have a collection of shapes in a bag and a matching set for everyone to see, then one child can feel and describe a shape hidden in the bag and the others can point to its partner
- **foil shapes**: cover shapes in foil, then remove them and challenge children to match the foil shell to the object and explain how they know

Designing and making things to fit a particular shape
Identifying shape similarities, fitting shapes together and making new shapes, visualising
For example, using interlocking 2D shapes, other construction resources or recycled material, such as a box for a toy, bed for a bear, a hat

Visualising shapes
Visualising shape properties from different viewpoints, manipulating shapes
For example, inviting the children to imagine being tiny and walking inside a Smarties tube, then asking, 'What shape will you see at the end?'

Focusing on spatial relations: position, directions and transformations

Shape puzzles
Using and visualising transformations

For example, rotating and flipping shapes to fit gaps, such as filling a frame or computer programs

Pattern making
Using rules, recognising spatial relationships, predicting results of transformations
For example, with different media, pattern kits and computer programs

- **printing** with various materials, noting patterns
- **weaving**, for example large scale through an outdoor fence
- **making reflective patterns** with reversals of position: kaleidoscopes, mirrors, dancing with a partner, peg boards divided in half, completing half a butterfly, Magic Mirror books (Walter 2000)

Designing a layout
Visualising and describing positions and directions
For example, 'landscape toys', roadways, tracks and trails for toy cars, trains, robots, trikes; children acting a familiar story outdoors (e.g. 'Billy Goats Gruff'); following an obstacle course, with a circuit of things to crawl through, jump over, walk on, slide down, weave between; solving maze puzzles

Giving and following instructions
Visualising, predicting and describing positions and directions
For example, to partners, robots, vehicles outdoors; treasure hunts with positional clues

10 Measuring

Teacher: How shall we measure these?
Amy: You need a measurer.
There was no ruler or measuring tape available in the nursery, so Amy decided to make one. She went off and found a stick and drew lots of lines and numbers on it.

A nursery acquired a lot of retractable measuring tapes: the children enthusiastically went around 'measuring' everything, by putting the tapes against things and saying numbers.

Although a long way from fully understanding the measuring process, these children knew that measuring involves using tools with numbers. Measuring is about giving numbers to things like length, weight or speed so they can be compared. This involves using units of measure and knowing what they are worth. Measures can be devised for a variety of properties like calories in food, shades of colours or the warmth of duvets. It can even be applied to entertainment, beauty and cleverness, by using stars or rating scales. In order to understand measuring, children must understand what is being measured, know the units and be able to use tools to obtain numbers. Understanding units of invisible properties like weight and time is difficult and the use of measuring tools can be problematic.

Piaget *et al.* (1960: 301) argued that children's difficulties depended on two key concepts: conservation and transitivity. Conservation, as discussed in relation to number, is the idea that an amount does not change, even if the appearance has altered, so long as nothing has been added or taken away. For instance, most six year olds will say there is more playdough when a ball is rolled out long and thin. As with numbers of objects, children are initially misled by the 'stretched out' appearance. Similarly, children believe that there is more liquid when it is poured into a taller container and that a lump of playdough weighs more when it is split into bits. Dickson *et al.* (1984) concluded that Piaget's progression was largely confirmed, with children understanding length first, followed by conservation of substance at about seven or eight (as with playdough) and weight not until nine or ten. Logically, conservation underpins measurement: if children think that an amount changes with its appearance, they cannot compare amounts in different situations.

In the classic Piagetian test for transitivity, young children who were asked to compare two towers of bricks some distance apart failed to use a stick to do so. They apparently did not understand the idea of a 'go between' to make an indirect comparison. The idea of transitivity is implicit in the use of units and is sometimes expressed as: if A > B and B > C then A > C. However, Nunes and Bryant (1996) reported that children under five readily used a stick to compare the depths of two holes. They also found that five year olds understood how to use units to compare amounts and realised that inches produced a different result than centimetres because they were larger. Dickson *et al.* concluded that children can learn measuring ideas before passing conservation tests and that teaching children how to measure might help them to understand conservation and transitivity.

These findings challenge the traditional teaching approach of comparing things directly, then indirectly, before using measuring tools, like rulers and scales. The traditional approach also introduced non-standard before standard units, for instance using handspans before centimetres. Showing that different handspans produced different results was supposed to help children appreciate the need to use standard units. However, Boulton-Lewis *et al.* (1996) found that children were unlikely to understand this idea until about eight or nine years of age, because of the complex reasoning involved, and younger children were more successful using standard units. According to Gussin Paley's (1981) account of five year olds measuring a carpet by using children lying down, they believed it was no longer possible to measure when one of the children was absent. They had difficulty understanding that any children could be used. Informal measuring methods therefore seem harder to understand than conventional ones. If children use standard units from the beginning, for instance by measuring their height in centimetres, they are also more likely to get a feel for units and to acquire 'benchmarks' for estimating (Ainley 1991). Certainly, it makes no sense to use non-standard units for time, yet age is the most important measure for young children. When Italian five and six year olds had to communicate measurements to a carpenter to make a table, they chose to use centimetres rather than shoes and did so successfully (Reggio Children 1997).

Children, like the 'measurers' above, want to use adult tools which are part of their culture, as Boulton-Lewis *et al.* (1996) found. From a Vygotskian stance, children benefit from an apprenticeship approach: by observing adults, 'role-playing' and being taught measuring, they become familiar with units and tools. They also build on their experiences of height charts, parents doing DIY and weighing vegetables in the supermarket. These will vary according to particular family interests and circumstances, like the children described in Chapter 3 who knew a lot about the weights of family members, pigeon racing or car speeds and journeys. These experiences are likely to foster children's interest and understanding of measures. One four year old, whose mother did a lot of baking, went home after making cookies at school and told her the weight in grams for all the ingredients. Nowadays, young children may have fewer experiences of some measures. With less home baking and more pre-packaged goods, it could be argued that measuring weight, volume and capacity is now less important. However, an understanding of measuring is still important for areas such as science, design and technology.

How does learning about measuring develop?

Although current approaches may recommend early experience, children's understanding will take many years to develop. Different areas of measurement, such as length, area, volume and capacity, weight and time, have particular difficulties associated with them.

Linear measurement

Dickson *et al.* (1984) reported that children under six thought that walking across a room in one direction was not the same distance as coming back. Some thought it was further one way and some the other: their opinions did not change when watching a doll walking instead. They also thought that it was further when running, because it was faster.

Length is the simplest and most visual measurement for children to understand. Units of length are used as images for numbers, with number lines and colour rods (where numbers are different lengths). However, as these examples show, children have significant difficulties with comparing length. Young children will compare their heights without first making sure that they are standing level (or taking their shoes off); they will run a race without appreciating the need for a level starting point. A traditional assessment of conservation is to align two pencils of the same length and then to move one forward. Young children will say the latter is now longer, because they only look at one end of each pencil. Considering both ends of both pencils is demanding for young children.

Language is another potential source of difficulty. Linear measurement occurs in a range of contexts, involving length, height, distance, width and depth, with a great range of vocabulary including long, tall, far, wide and deep and their opposites, short, near, narrow and shallow. Comparative terms like 'taller than' and 'tallest' can cause difficulty, with some children tending to say 'taller and'.

Children's use of manipulable units like cubes can reveal their understanding. If they do not realise what is being measured, they may leave gaps or fail to cover the whole distance. However, young children can begin to use units: with a programmable robot, they estimate the number of units of its own length required to go a certain distance. Five year olds can reason that a ribbon three inches long would be longer than one three centimetres long and can show what 'four centimetres long' is on a ruler (Nunes and Bryant, 1996). However, when five and six year olds were asked to put numbers on a marked ruler, some children wrote numbers in a string without paying any attention to the marks or equal spacing. Most children did not start from 0, but put '1' against the mark at the ruler's edge, implying they were counting the lines rather than the spaces between them. When given rulers which were wrongly drawn, most children did not think it was important to put '1' at the end of the first centimetre rather than before. I once asked an eight year old to show me a centimetre on a metre rule: she pointed to one of the 'hash' marks and explained that each line was a centimetre. Clements and Stephan (2004: 301) concluded that, for young children, 'the numerals on the ruler signify when to start counting, not an amount of space that has been covered'. They recommended the use of centimetre cubes, which seem more relevant than using non-standard cubes to measure the growth of beanplants, for instance. Interlocking centimetre cubes in sticks of ten can help children understand rulers and provide a context for counting larger numbers. An understanding of rulers is important because they are the simplest examples of measuring scales, as on a variety of measuring instruments, such as thermometers.

Capacity

> *With some five year olds, I filled up a tall thin pot and a short fat one, and then emptied the tall pot into four cups and the short one into six cups. 'So which pot holds more?' I asked. 'The tall pot,' they replied, explaining that it was taller. I then asked, 'How many cups did we get out of this one? And that one? Which is more, six or four?' The children answered correctly. When I asked again, 'So which pot holds more?' they promptly repeated, 'The tall one!'*

Young children seem to have an affinity with capacity, as they enjoy filling and emptying containers: however, they often seem focused on pouring. Most will have difficulty with conservation. Baratta-Lorton (1976) recommended that children should empty the same jug into a variety of tall and shallow containers, mark the level on each and then discuss why they are different.

The concepts and language of capacity and volume are complex. A vacuum flask has a much smaller capacity than the space it takes up on the shelf, while a cornflake box always has a much greater capacity than the volume of cereal inside. Children do not understand volume, or how much space something takes up, before they are 11 or 12, according to conservation tests (Dickson *et al.* 1984). Capacity refers to the amount a container potentially holds. 'Holds more than' is a difficult phrase for young children, compared with 'longer' or 'heavier'. Other vocabulary which children must learn in order to compare capacity includes 'full' and 'overflows', as well as more familiar phrases like 'filling up' and 'fitting in'.

Children may have misconceptions when comparing capacity directly: if a large jug is emptied into a smaller one, the latter overflows. Children sometimes say that the smaller jug holds more, perhaps because there is more water around. Harrison (1987) pointed out that children may confuse 'fullness' with capacity, thinking that the fuller container holds more. This seems related to the misconception that there is more water in a taller container because the water level is higher. One reason why expensive liquids like perfume and wine are usually sold in tall thin bottles is that comparing three dimensions simultaneously is challenging even for adults.

With units, young children can predict that it will take longer to fill up a flower pot with a teaspoon than with a trowel, and some can estimate how many jugfuls are needed to fill the water tray. Children can compare capacity with a variety of materials, including beads and beans, which raises the issue of whether the spaces between make any difference. There are two kinds of standard units for capacity, such as cubic centimetres and millilitres, which is potentially confusing. Children's home experiences may include cooking, petrol stations and lifts, where the capacity is also expressed in 'persons'.

Weight

> *I once inadvertently contributed to children's confusion by providing objects to sort into 'heavy' and 'light', which included things like a sponge and a white feather. When a child explained he had put the objects in the 'light' set because they were pale coloured, I realised that I needed to include dark coloured light objects.*

Children can find weight difficult because it is invisible. A common misconception is that larger things weigh more, so children need to discuss large light things and small heavy things.

Fielker (1976) pointed out the difficulties with weighing scales: using balances requires some understanding. With bucket scales young children often think the aim is to fill one side so that it crashes down. Judging when scales are level can be difficult, and sometimes involves matching up small vertical lines on the stand. It is not obvious to young children that 'down' means heavier. One four year old had a battery which he maintained was heavier than any other object: when a heavy stone made his battery go up on the scales, he insisted that 'up' meant heavier. A seesaw can introduce young children to these ideas. Using hands to compare weights is not reliable: the object requiring least resistance feels lighter, which may be due to the muscles of one forearm being stronger. Swapping hands can just result in confusion. A further complication involves pressure: large objects feel lighter than small ones of the same weight. (This is why an elephant standing on one foot exerts less pressure than a stiletto heel.)

Children can begin comparing weights of objects in paper bags, with their arms down. Baratta-Lorton (1976) recommended an informal spring balance, with an open box suspended on elastic. (Some teachers use a string bag on interlocked rubber bands.) Putting a sheet of paper behind to mark levels allows a scale to be recorded. This approach focuses on weight as the downward pull of gravity, before comparing two weights. Children can predict how far objects will be pulled down, revealing their understanding. Later, children will need to distinguish scientific concepts of mass from weight. However, as mass is experienced as weight on this planet, and 'weight' is the everyday expression, this distinction seems unnecessary for young children. As mentioned previously, young children's experience of weight will relate to specific experiences, including weighing people and moving heavy objects.

Area

Whereas Piaget claimed that children understood conservation of area at about the same time as length, this is now disputed, according to Clements and Stephan (2004). Young children have difficulty accepting that a shape cut up and rearranged still has the same area. When comparing the area of shapes, they tend just to consider one side. They also have difficulty in covering surfaces up to the boundaries and with no gaps, so experience of this may be useful. Zacharos and Ravanis (2000) found that children over six could measure area more successfully with the familiar context of fitting cars into car parks. However, in order to measure area, children have to cover surfaces in rows and columns and to begin to understand multiplication. They then need to connect this with linear measurement. Thus understanding area involves complex ideas.

Time

Four year old: I'm going to do this till home time!
Friend: [aghast] You'll miss tidy-up time and story time!

Piaget (1969) suggested that children could not sequence events until they were seven or eight. However, four year olds like these above have a clear idea of the order of events in the nursery session. Understanding may vary greatly depending on experiences at home: some children's parents will mention time much more frequently than others.

Kerslake (1975) found that children did not understand telling the time until they were about eight. Children could be trained to read a clock without any awareness of the time of day or any concept of a minute or an hour. However, telling the time involves many concepts and skills, such as knowing the different functions of the hands, reading numerals, understanding a 'clockwise' direction, counting in multiples of five and recognising fractions of a turn. According to Dickson *et al.* (1984), five year olds' difficulties in telling the time are related to numerals and counting.

Measuring time has two aspects: position and duration. The first involves sequencing events and identifying particular times. For instance, a question beginning 'When . . .?' may be answered with 'Before . . .' or 'After . . .,' or with 'Four o' clock,' 'Tuesday' or '1984.' Dickson *et al.* reported that some three year olds could say their age and answer questions about what they would do tomorrow or when they went to bed (for instance, 'after watching television'). They tended to confuse yesterday and tomorrow, saying, 'I'm going to nan's yesterday.' Five year olds may know their age at their next birthday and the days of the week, and the times of things they do regularly. Children therefore need to relate telling the time to meaningful times of their day, such as when they go to bed or watch television, even if these are not 'o' clock' times.

Duration is implied by questions beginning with 'How long?' This involves measuring units and calculating the differences between times on a clock or calendar. Apart from being invisible, time is very subjectively experienced, with a minute in one context feeling much longer than another, which makes estimating time difficult. Kerslake argued that children understood this aspect least. She recommended timing activities, beginning with seconds and minutes, which are more comprehensible than hours. Timing turns on trikes or computers, how long children take to do things or how many actions they can perform in a minute can be done with sand-timers or kitchen-timers (which have the advantage of showing the number of minutes and also ringing).

The most significant measure for most children is their age, suggesting the value of activities relating to birthdays. One three year old asked her nursery teacher how to write three and a half, perhaps prompted by siblings' discussion of ages: she then wrote three crosses, possibly as 'halves'. Carr (1992) suggested that children saw number lines in terms of ages, helping them to identify the age they will be next. Alan, when he was four and asked his age, seemed engaged by this idea: 'I'm nearly three; no, I'm nearly six, no, I'm nearly seven!' A number line showing halves might help some children express their age more precisely.

Young-Loveridge (1989) found that some four year old 'number experts' had many conversations about time at home. Some had learned to recognise numerals from the clock. They were at various stages of telling the time, but all had used the calendar to count down to birthdays and Christmas, some counting nights as a number of 'sleeps'. This suggests that discussions about time may help number understanding.

It therefore seems important to discuss time with children in terms of the significant events and times of their day, relating to sequence and how long they must wait. Experiences such as advent calendars may help children with the concept of a day, as well as names of days of the week. Five year olds can be very interested in making zig-zag books which describe familiar processes, such as cooking or tie-dying, often returning repeatedly to rehearse the sequences. Some are also interested in timetables, which help give a picture of the day, so they know what is going to happen. Five year olds' understanding of time can be revealed by asking them to draw a clock which they know. Some children may not realise how many numbers there are, how they are arranged, or even that clocks have numbers not letters, while others may demonstrate knowledge of different hands or minute marks (Pengelly 1985).

Money

Money is a measure, and possibly the most difficult to understand, as it involves measuring the value of things, a very nebulous idea. Young children seem to expect that one item should be exchanged for one penny, as in the shopping game described in Chapter 7. They are not keen to accept a five pence coin instead of five pennies. However, this equivalence cannot be physically demonstrated as with length. Dickson *et al.* (1984) pointed out the complex skills and understanding involved with money:

- Coin recognition: involving size, colour of metal, number. This is largely dependent on the amount of experience children have had with real coins.
- Relative value: knowing 5p is worth more than 2p but less than 10p involves being able to compare numbers, and also metals, with silver worth more than copper. Size values are confusing, as 5p is smaller than 2p.
- Unit value: a 10p coin is worth ten pennies, taking these as the basic unit.
- Other equivalences: knowing a ten pence coin is also equivalent to two 5ps and five 2ps.

Understanding equivalence with money therefore involves conservation, counting, numeral recognition, ordering, addition, doubling and halving, and number bonds. It also seems dependent on children's experiences of exchange in real shopping contexts, which, as noted earlier, is declining for young children in the UK. Understanding addition and change with coins depends on all of this. Dickson *et al.* concluded that money is not a good context for introducing children to number, as is sometimes recommended, because it requires a great deal of prior understanding.

The implications are that money experiences are helpful if they are as realistic as possible, involving the exchange of things of equivalent value. Rather than pricing things unrealistically in pennies, a pound shop may be more appropriate for young children. If they are to learn the value of coins, then real money is essential: requiring children to match coins on to silhouettes on a card can help check none is lost. Real pennies are also cheaper than plastic coins.

Role-play with various businesses and services can relate to children's experiences with money, including boot fairs or bus tickets. One nursery set up an outdoor market: however, children only wrote the names of things when making price labels, suggesting that prices were not significant to them (echoing previous research, Rogers 1996). Price tags were then arranged to face customers so they had to read them to the adult stall holders. It is therefore important to link play with visits to real shops and markets. Some schools run 'tuck' shops selling fruit which involve the children; raising money for charity with cake or plant sales also provides realistic experience of money.

Activities for measures

Measuring brings together many aspects of number, shape and space. It also demonstrates a major use of mathematics in adult life, both everyday, with time and money, and in many aspects of production and services, science, design and technology. Young children can become familiar with measuring practices while gradually gaining understanding by processes such as comparing, predicting and explaining unexpected results. Activities which involve making things to fit, like a bed for the teddy (see Fig. 10.1), prompt children to compare lengths.

The following list summarises the main opportunities for children to practise measuring.

Design and technology activities: making hats, beds, houses, garages, bookbags

Finding things which are the same or different: making different patterns with equal lengths; finding containers which are the same or the odd one out

Making deliberate mistakes: comparing heights with someone standing on a box; measuring from the wrong place on the ruler

Asking children to draw rulers or clocks

Predicting: guessing and counting how many fit in the jar; what will happen with the scales; how many jugs will fill the water tray

Blockplay: finding pairs the same length to make a window; substituting two blocks for a longer block

Figure 10.1 A bed for the teddy

Stories: *You'll Soon Grow Into Them, Titch* (Hutchins 1983); *Jim and the Beanstalk* (Briggs 1973); *I Am Not Sleepy and I Will Not Go to Bed* (Child 2001)

Role-play: shops, markets, boot fairs, DIY store, baby clinics, garden centre

Robots: estimating the number of units to make Roamer knock down the skittles

Children's height with metres and centimetres

Cooking: using standard measures and tools; using spoonfuls and cupfuls; weighing flour with eggs

Growing things: experimenting with the amount of water needed; time taken to flower

Science investigations: how far cars go down a ramp; melting times in different conditions

Timing, with kitchen timers or clocks: how long children take to tidy up, get changed, line up or sit down; how many jumps or circuits they can do in a minute; turns on trikes or computers

'Advent' calendars: how long until the party, the eggs hatch, a birthday, the holidays

11 Problem solving

Fadilah (a good counter, aged four) was tackling a sharing problem involving three teddy bears of different sizes and 12 sweets.

Teacher:	*How many teddies?*
Fadilah:	*[counts] 1, 2, 3*
T:	*Can you count the sweets?*
F:	*[counts 12 sweets correctly]*
T:	*Can you share them?*
F:	*[Lots of taking away and rearranging until the little bear had all the sweets]*
T:	*Is that fair?*
F:	*Yes, because the other two have been naughty.*
T:	*What did they do?*
F:	*They hit her.*
G:	*Oh look, there is another bear. Can she have any sweets?*
F:	*She can only have one because she hit her too!*

Fadilah was the youngest of three siblings.

Fadilah clearly saw sharing in terms of social justice rather than mathematical equality. The problem was one we were trying out as part of the Number in Early Childhood project (Gifford 1995). Teachers found that if the bears were different sizes children focused on this: 'If the little bear has the same as the others it will be sick!' or 'The fat bear is on a diet!' Even in 'real life' contexts children did not engage with the intended mathematical problem. For example, when asked to share real biscuits, they sometimes grabbed and made no attempt to share fairly, suggesting that their view of the problem was to get as many as possible. Some teachers decided it was more honest to ask, 'Would you like to solve a maths problem?' and found that children would engage readily in nonsensical tasks like sharing plastic bears between plates. As these examples suggest, trying to engage young children in mathematical problem solving can be problematic.

What does mathematical problem solving look like for three to fives?

Problem solving comes in many sizes and guises: problems can be quite minor and arise incidentally from activities or be part of major projects. They may be posed by children themselves, as in blockplay, where children regularly set themselves the problem of building the biggest arch possible (Gura 1992). Children may decide to make something for collaborative play, such as the car pictured in Fig. 11.1, or be inspired by stories, as with Farrah's houses for the three bears (see Figs 11.2–11.4). These involve mathematics such as choosing

Figure 11.1 A car

-Farrah 15ᵗʰ Nov ʔ0

Figure 11.2 Farrah's houses for the three bears (drawn by an adult)

shapes according to their properties, deciding how to place them, and in Farrah's case, representing in different ways.

Sometimes design projects may be adult-initiated, such as planning a wild garden or a new role-play area. I planned a party with a reception class who used data handling strategies to decide activities and refreshments, resulting in a novel party which involved 'tennis'. On a smaller scale, children may set up a party in the home-corner and solve the problem of getting the right number of plates either by putting one plate for each person or by counting people then plates. Problem solving is also intrinsic to some apparatus, games or puzzles. For instance, Deloache and Brown (1987) found that two year olds would spontaneously set about putting nesting cups in order. With

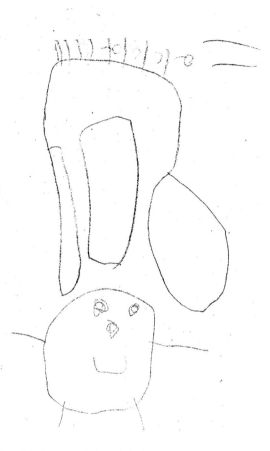

Figure 11.3   Farrah's drawing of a bear in its house

games, decoding dice numerals is a problem which children solved by using a number frieze either to count pictures or to count the symbols (see Fig. 11.5).

Fadilah's problem was a version of that posed to four and five year olds by Davis and Pepper (1992), whose findings demonstrated some key aspects of problem solving and children's strategies. Twelve biscuits were shared between two dolls: children generally used a 'dealing action schema' of giving one biscuit to each doll in turn, so they had six each. In the 'redistribution' problem, a third doll comes along, who must get an even share before any biscuits are eaten. The

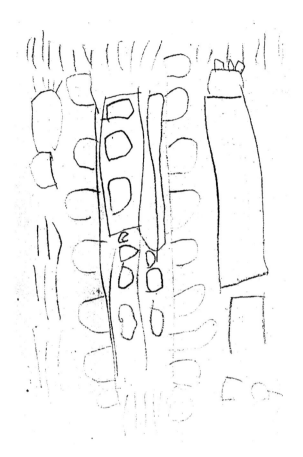

Figure 11.4   Farrah's plan view of the construction

children then used a range of strategies to give each doll four biscuits. Some children gathered up the biscuits and dealt them all out again; most did some complicated giving and readjusting. Two children crumbled up all the biscuits and redistributed them as a pile of crumbs each, which the researchers conceded was a successful solution. Some children, including those who were not good counters, seemed to 'just see' a solution, and gave two biscuits from each doll to the third doll.

Davis and Pepper considered this a genuine problem for two reasons: it required 'cogitation' rather than an automatic response

Figure 11.5 Decoding numbers using a number frieze

like 'dealing'; and there were so many strategies (19 among 74 children, most successful) that children could not be using a learned method. The National Curriculum (DfEE/QCA 1999) characterised mathematical problem solving as presenting difficulties and involving decisions about approaches and materials. Challenge and choice of method are therefore key characteristics of problems. If children know or are told the method to use, then they are not problem solving.

Why is problem solving important?

Problem solving has been advocated as a major vehicle for learning by Piaget (1973) and Vygotsky (1978), who emphasised collaborative and guided problem solving. In overcoming difficulties children have to connect what they know to new situations. For instance, with the arch problem, children often began by holding an upright and the crosspiece, but found they needed another hand for the third block. Some solved this by finding a friend. Others realised that you could place the two uprights first. Then, wanting to make a large arch, they would place the uprights too far apart, so the crosspiece fell between them. Some children solved the problem by using a 'spacer', which matched the top block, to place under the uprights. The children discovered different ways of making an arch, varying sequence, position, number and length of blocks. Problem solving like this can encourage children to make new connections with existing knowledge and, as Piaget implied, provides motivation for learning. It involves all the major cognitive learning processes, in visualising solutions, checking for errors, and in a collaborative context, imitation and instruction as well as talking and reflecting. It also involves metacognition in evaluating strategies and solutions. Deloache and Brown (1987) described children trying to balance blocks of wood on a metal beam, who persisted in finding a single method to include trick blocks with hidden weights. They called this 'theorising' since the children took feedback into account in order to revise previous theories (such as finding the middle of the blocks). Problem solving can therefore stimulate higher level thinking, including the analysis of problems, synthesis of relevant ideas and creativity when unusual solutions are found, as with the children who redistributed the biscuits as crumbs.

Problem solving also involves important emotional and social learning. Successful problem solving enhances self-esteem and can help children to develop 'mastery orientation'. The children who planned the party became more confident and were keen to tackle new projects. Collaborative problem solving can help forge relationships, giving emotional as well as cognitive support. However, this requires social skills such as gaining entry, giving and taking advice, and resolving disagreements (Broadhead 2004). Moreover, problem solving by definition is difficult and can also threaten self-esteem. Adults therefore have a key role in fostering a supportive climate for problem solving.

What do we know about how young children solve problems?

Research reviewing problem solving in mathematics suggests that young children employ similar strategies to older ones. The difference lies in their expertise in the area (Askew and Wiliam 1995). Deloache and Brown (1987) found the following sequence of approaches, for two to three year olds with nesting cups and for four to seven year olds making a train-track circuit:

- brute force: trying to hammer bits so that they fit
- local correction: adjusting one part, often creating a different problem
- dismantling: starting all over again
- holistic review: considering multiple relations or simultaneous adjustments, such as repairing by insertion and reversal.

'Brute force' is a strategy familiar to anyone who has watched young children trying to solve puzzles. Davis and Pepper's redistribution problem provides further examples: those who crumbled the biscuits used 'brute force'; some children got into cycles of 'local corrections' by taking too many from one doll and then having to give back from another; others 'dismantled' and started again. The children who used fewest moves may have considered multiple relations, taking all dolls into account at once. Those who 'just saw' the solution may have considered the problem as a whole.

Askew and Wiliam reported that older children planned first, while four year olds tended to start solving practical problems immediately. However, Gura (1992) found that blockplay planning depended on experience rather than age. Deloache and Brown found three year olds used planning to find a hidden toy: when they had to wait before they could start searching, they rehearsed verbally or by looking repeatedly. They reported three year olds looking for a lost camera, who used systematic strategies and searched only in places visited since it was last seen. Some young children, when problem solving, explore possibilities very systematically. One child trying on hats in the nursery hat shop methodically sorted those tried from those untried. Similarly, a five year old ordering fruit by weight carefully separated heavier from lighter after each weighing. Children choosing numbers to add often progress systematically using a pattern of 1 + 1, 2 + 2, 3 + 3. Marion Bird (1991) reported five year olds recording numerical and spatial investigations systematically. The children collecting data for the party showed systems such as making lists when asking who had a tennis racket. Questions like 'How could we make it easier for someone to understand?' can help children to organise their recording.

Successful problem solvers' strategies therefore include:

- getting a feel for the problem, looking at it holistically, checking they have understood, for example talking it through or asking questions
- planning, preparing and predicting outcomes, for example gathering blocks together before building
- monitoring progress towards the goal, for example checking that the bear will fit the bed.
- being systematic, trying possibilities methodically without repetition, rather than at random, for example separating shapes tried from those not tried in a puzzle
- trying alternative approaches and evaluating strategies, for example trying different positions for shapes
- refining and improving solutions, for example solving a puzzle again in fewer moves.

These strategies involve reflection and awareness of thinking. Teachers can help this by modelling strategies and encouraging children to talk about their methods. Children also need a repertoire of alternative methods to choose from, implying a range of expertise. They also need the confidence to be flexible, to be familiar with tackling problems and using what they know. All of this requires support from adults.

Problem contexts and levels of difficulty

Fadilah's response may have been influenced by the difficulty of the problem, prompting her to reinterpret it. Carr (2001) described children reframing challenges to reduce the difficulty, for instance making a hat for an imaginary character instead of a specific toy to avoid measuring. Carr *et al.* (1994) suggested that three things affected the level of difficulty for mathematical enterprises:

- familiar contexts
- meaningful purposes
- mathematical complexity.

For Fadilah, the context clearly resonated. However, children from less advantaged backgrounds can find contextualised problems harder than abstract problems (Jordan *et al.* 2003; Cooper and Dunne 2004). Children perform best in contexts which are culturally familiar to them from home practices, according to Boulton-Lewis (1990). She found that aboriginal children in Australia demonstrated their mathematical potential best in problems about family relationships or playing cards. However, Deloache and Brown (1987) argued for age-appropriate contexts. They found it was only when researchers used hide and seek contexts that young children displayed planning and systematic search strategies, while four to seven year olds displayed theorising and persistence when balancing blocks of wood. Contexts therefore need to be carefully chosen: people of any age 'can display more sophisticated cognition when reasoning about familiar than unfamiliar matters', according to Deloache and Brown (1987: 109).

Purpose may have been a problem for Fadilah: she may simply not have cared about sharing the sweets. Children may be more likely to engage with problems that they have set themselves, like making a car or a satisfying pattern. Deloache and Brown asked about the cups and blocks, 'Why does the child bother?' and concluded that so long as children are 'interested in the outcome and understand the goal even two year olds actively and systematically pursue the solution' (1987: 119). The key factor may be ownership rather than who initiated the problem. Carr *et al.* argued that the child has to have control of the outcome or else they may just look for the right answer to please the teacher. 'Understanding the goal' also implies that language may be an issue: Fadilah may not have thought that sharing meant equality.

Mathematical difficulty may also have been an issue for Fadilah, although she was a good counter. Children who are not confident in problem solving will generally fall back on less efficient but more secure strategies, according to Boulton-Lewis. This throws doubt on whether it is possible for children to 'use *developing* mathematical ideas and methods' to solve problems, as in the Early Learning Goals (DfEE/QCA 2000). People seem to need a secure understanding in order to use mathematical methods to solve problems. For instance, children who do not count reliably are unlikely to use counting to find the number of a group.

For children to engage in mathematical problem solving, it therefore seems that they need problems:

- which they understand – in familiar contexts
- where the outcomes matter to them
- where they have control of the process
- which involve mathematics with which they are confident.

How can teachers help?

Gura (1992) noted that some children are more likely to pose problems than others. A problem posing leader can provide opportunities for other children to collaboratively tackle projects like building palaces and roads, which give rise to whole series of problems. Broadhead (2004) argued that long periods of uninterrupted time were necessary for such play to develop and children might need support in developing the necessary social skills.

'Problem solving' in general is difficult to teach, but children can be taught to use strategies involving mathematical ideas, according to Askew and Wiliam (1995). For instance, adults can teach children to check using counting and can provide strategies for puzzles and computer games. Scaffolding can support problem solving: as discussed in Chapter 6, this involves providing support contingent on the child's responses, such as breaking the problem down into smaller steps and drawing children's attention to key features. Coltman *et al.* (2002) gave children clues, such as suggesting they looked more closely at all the faces of the shape when trying to match a solid to a 2D shape.

Questioning is a key strategy to focus children's attention, but more subtle strategies such as a comment or look can be effective, as with the adult handing Seema the block to begin her tower at the top. In the Reggio table measuring project (Reggio Children 1997), the teachers used more proactive methods and gathered the children together at intervals during the project, to give them a lesson on non-standard measures or to discuss and vote on alternative methods. Asking children to talk about and show what they have done helps them to analyse and review the situation. Coltman *et al.* found that encouraging children to check meant they later did this themselves. Burton (1984) suggested that, with older children, 'self-organising' questions were useful: these are questions which children can use as prompts. Examples for different stages of a problem might be:

Getting to grips:	*What are we trying to do?*
Connecting to previous experience:	*Have we done anything like this before?*
Planning:	*What do we need?*
Considering alternative methods:	*Is there another way?*
Monitoring progress:	*How does it look so far?*
Evaluating solutions:	*Does it work?*
	How can we check?
	Could we make it even better?

Curtis' (1998) conclusion that adults who modelled curious, questioning behaviour encouraged this in children suggests that modelling attitudes may be as important as teaching strategies. Adults who acknowledge difficulties and being 'stuck' but who also demonstrate perseverance can help children to persist and become positive problem solvers. Further suggestions for general problem solving are offered by advocates of thinking skills (see, for instance, www.thinkingskills.com).

Different kinds of problems

Askew (2003: 85) quotes Burkhard's taxonomy of problems:

- action problems, 'the solution to which may directly affect everyday life'

- believable problems, hypothetical or story problems
- curious problems, 'which intrigue'
- dubious problems, 'existing only to provide dressed up exercises'
- educational problems, 'essentially dubious' but which make an important point.

This suggests a framework for providing opportunities for mathematical problem solving. 'Action problems' seems a more appropriate category than 'real life', since it can include children's problems involved in play, which is real to them. Experienced educators may plan 'curious problems', knowing what is likely to 'hook' young children. These may involve matching shapes to holes for younger children or counting large numbers for older ones, as with the children who wanted to know how many stars were on the wall in their spaceship area. 'Dubious problems' or exercises, if they offer no choice or responsibility, are not problems at all. With 'educational problems', teachers can expose muddles for children to resolve. Swan (2003: 117) described using problems to reveal inconsistencies and create cognitive conflict, by discussing children's unaided attempts at problems, calling this 'teaching for meaning'. For instance, when planning the party, I asked the children how they would decide what cakes to cook. They said, 'Ask us and we'll put our hands up.' This resulted in most children putting their hands up for most options, leaving them none the wiser. The children then realised that a more systematic approach was needed, involving recording. I could have organised this for the children, but the muddle posed a problem which helped make an important point about data collection. Different kinds of problem solving can therefore provide a range of learning experiences for children and can provide an effective teaching strategy to assess and clarify misconceptions and to increase understanding.

Opportunities for mathematical problem solving

The following lists provide some suggestions for problem solving contexts, which will involve most of the learning processes.

Adult-initiated

- Preparing: checking there is enough for everyone, for example plates or brushes
- Sharing: checking everyone has the same amount
- Tidying up: organising storage and checking nothing has been lost
- Gardening: arranging plants and bulbs, predicting their growth
- Voting for stories, songs, games or activities
- Planning and setting up: a wild garden or new role-play area
- Communicating: plans, measurements, invitations with times and maps.

Child-initiated

- Construction play and model-making materials: finding like shapes, fitting things together, checking sizes
- Pattern-making materials: creating patterns with rules, using shape properties, movements and positions
- Drawing and picture-making materials; making shapes to represent things
- Open-ended role-play areas: the 'whatever you want it to be place' (Broadhead 2004, for children to construct their own scenarios)
- Mathematical tools for children to use in play, for example calendars for making appointments, calculators for working out prices, scales for weighing a baby.

Games and puzzles

- Turn-taking games with numeral dice
- Nesting, ordering, matching, fitting shapes, for example jig-saws and posting boxes
- Matching numerals and pictures, ordering numerals on a 'washing line'
- Computer games for numbers, directions, shapes
- Hiding games: feely bags with shapes, 'Bears in the Box' game
- Scoring games in children's own ways
- Open-ended game materials, for example pennies, buttons,

shells, dinosaurs, dice, spinners, small containers and 'empty tracks'.

Stories for problem posing

- Invented stories, such as 'Susie's treasures' in Chapter 6
- Adapted versions of books such as *The Doorbell Rang* (Hutchins 1986) or *The Great Pet Sale* (Inkpen 1998)
- Robots as story characters or transport, for example Postman Pat's van delivering letters
- Making settings for stories with small world toys or construction apparatus.

Conclusion

Considering how children learn different aspects of mathematics in a holistic way, with and from other people, in structured and open-ended situations, makes some points clear and also raises some issues and areas for development.

Young children can learn mathematics

Rather than waiting until children are ready to understand ideas before introducing them, it seems that children need time to become familiar with numbers, shapes or measuring tools before they can understand them. They need to practise counting so that it becomes automatic before they can understand the value of numbers. When they are familiar with the shapes of building blocks, they can then use them in more varied ways and make more complex structures and patterns. Children therefore need opportunities and encouragement to become familiar and to practise if they are to investigate and generalise relationships and apply mathematics to problem solving, such as using counting to see if shares are fair.

Young children enjoy engaging with mathematics

'Mathematics is everywhere' used to be the mantra, and the sign of a successful activity was that 'the children didn't even realise they were doing maths!' However, it seems that mathematics in everyday contexts may be hard for teachers and children to identify. Young children do find mathematics focused activities interesting, enjoyable and relevant. They are excited by large numbers, fascinated by zero and enjoy matching shapes and spotting patterns. They feel satisfied when they have learned to count or recognise numbers and when these skills are valued by their families. They make jokes out of errors and enjoy ludicrous possibilities, such as impossibly large amounts. They enjoy exploring different possibilities and arrangements and using shape and space properties to create visual harmony. They rise to the challenge of solving problems and puzzles, like 'guess the hidden number' games. Some create new methods and solutions to problems, or enjoy recording in their own way. Mathematics therefore does not have to be hidden or embedded in utilitarian purposes in order to be relevant to young children. Engaging with ideas in a focused way may also make it easier for children and adults to see opportunities for mathematics in different contexts.

The role of adults is vital

Adults are important to foster children's interest and enthusiasm for learning and to create a safe risk taking environment, modelling attitudes such as curiosity or persistence. They are experts who are needed to demonstrate, model and instruct those aspects of maths which cannot be learned by practical exploration, like counting or measuring. They also have an important role in helping children see what they are learning, by providing language, focusing on feedback and encouraging reasoning. Developing language to discuss shape properties or number relationships, like 'same as' and 'more than', helps children to focus on these. Encouraging children to talk about what they have done helps them to be aware of their thinking, of why they chose certain shapes or how they counted. When adults point out to children the effects of their actions, such as how counting helped them to compare, or how turning the shape round made it taller, then children start to make connections and to apply their understanding.

Adult-initiated activities do not have to be adult directed

Both adult-led and child-initiated activities are important for learning mathematics. With young children, less directive, non-confrontational teaching strategies are effective as they allow children to be more actively engaged and in control. Teachers need a repertoire of different interactive approaches, which take account of the much greater imbalance of power between younger children and adults and foster and protect their self-esteem. Teaching mathematics to three to five year olds therefore involves:

- 'just being there' as a supportive play partner
- being a conversationalist, negotiating meanings and speculating, 'I wonder why?'
- being a collaborative problem solver, modelling attitudes and strategies
- leading activities, but 'giving autonomy' in choices and control
- being playful, by telling stories, using puppets, making deliberate mistakes, playing with ideas and joking mathematically.

What children might not know and might learn

Some curriculum guidelines are very broad and it takes children a long time to move from one step to the next. Identifying the components of understanding helps teachers to identify learning and to plan. Identifying things children might not realise helps teachers to prevent misconceptions. For instance, adults can demonstrate that counting from right to left works as well as from left to right. They can encourage children to investigate different possibilities with shapes and numbers, so they realise that shapes look different when turned round, or that five is still five in different arrangements. A more detailed knowledge of children's possible 'learning trajectories' therefore helps teachers to structure activities and capitalise on opportunities.

We do not know how children learn mathematics

Knowing 'how children learn mathematics' depends partly on how we see mathematics and learning: both are complex and fluid ideas. Learning will vary for individuals over time and in different situations, but some processes, factors involved and possible lines of development have been suggested. However, there are many crucial developments in learning mathematics which are not understood. For instance, we do not know what non-verbal images of number young children have, how they combine these with counting and how they develop abstract concepts. We do not know how children's visual images of shape relate to their understanding of properties. Teachers' observations of how children learn and think mathematically therefore provide valuable insights.

How should we teach mathematics to three to five year olds?

Teaching approaches implicitly depend on values. Here, it has been proposed that children should be considered as learning holistically, so teaching involves taking emotional, social and physical aspects into account. This means valuing children's interest in their own learning, being sensitive to their concerns and building on their strengths. For instance, children have a facility for visualising, which could be developed. We know that they can subitise or recognise numbers without counting and this has implications for understanding cardinality and great potential for seeing numbers as made up in different ways. We also know that children can subitise numbers by hearing, that music helps memory and that rhythmical actions help counting, which has implications for learning with music and dance. Some ways of learning seem promising, but we need to study them more. For instance, children can represent mathematics and numbers in their own ways, but it is not clear how this relates to standard forms of recording. Children are motivated by technological resources, including robots and software which encourage reasoning, but it seems unclear how to develop this in educational settings. There are many approaches to learning mathematics, such as through stories or outdoors, which can be developed further.

Teaching mathematics to three to five year olds is therefore a challenge in many ways. Observing children's concerns and ways of learning, combined with a knowledge of early mathematics, suggests new and appropriate ways of teaching, which involve subtlety, skill and playfulness.

References

Ainley, J. (1991). Is there any mathematics in measurement? In D. Pimm and E. Love (eds) *Teaching and Learning School Mathematics*. London, Hodder & Stoughton / Open University: 69–76.

Anghileri, J. and Baron, S. (1999). 'Playing with the materials of study: poleidoblocs.' *Education 3–13* **27**(2): 57–64.

Anning, A. (2002). 'Conversations around young children's drawing: the impact of the beliefs of significant others at home and school.' *The International Journal of Art and Design Education* **21**(3): 197–208.

Anning, A. and Edwards, A. (1999). *Promoting Children's Learning from Birth to Five: Developing the New Early Years Professional*. Buckingham, Open University Press.

Ansari, D. and Karmiloff-Smith, A. (2002). 'Atypical trajectories of number development: a neuroconstructivist perspective.' *Trends in Cognitive Sciences* **6**(12): 511–516.

Ashcraft, M. H., Kirk, E. P. and Hopko, D. (1998). On the cognitive consequences of mathematics anxiety. In C. Donlan (ed.) *The Development of Mathematical Skills*. Hove, East Sussex, Psychology Press Ltd: 175–196.

Askew, M. (2003). Word problems: Cinderellas or wicked witches? In I. Thompson (ed.) *Enhancing Primary Mathematics Teaching*. Maidenhead, Open University Press: 78–85.

Askew, M., Brown, M., Rhodes, V., Wiliam, D. and Johnson, D. (1997). *Effective Teachers of Numeracy: Report of a Study Carried Out for the Teacher Training Agency*. London, King's College, University of London.

Askew, M. and Wiliam, D. (1995). *Recent Research in Mathematics Education 5–16*. London, HMSO.

Athey, C. (ed.) (1990). *Extending Thought in Young Children: A Parent–Teacher Partnership*. London, Paul Chapman Publishing Ltd.

Aubrey, C. (1993). 'An investigation of the mathematical knowledge and competencies which young children bring into school.' *British Educational Research Journal* **19**(1): 27–41.

Aubrey, C. (2003). 'Count me in! Taking in early mathematical experiences.' *Primary Mathematics* Autumn: 17–20.

Aubrey, C., Bottle, G. and Godfrey, R. (2003). 'Early mathematics in the home and out-of-home contexts.' *International Journal of Early Years Education* **11**(2): 91–103.

Aubrey, C., Kavkler, M., Tancig, S. and Magajna, L. (2000). 'Getting it right from the start? The influence of early school entry on later achievements in mathematics.' *European Early Childhood Education Research Journal* **8**(1): 75–85.

Baker, D. (in press). Researching Home and School Mathematics Practices in the Early Years: a case study from the UK. *Home School Numeracy Practices*, Kluwer.

Baker, D., Street, B. and Tomlin, A. (2003). 'Mathematics as social: understanding relationships between home and school numeracy practices.' *For the Learning of Mathematics* **23**(3): 11–20.

Baratta-Lorton, M. (1976). *Mathematics Their Way*. Menlo Park, California, Addison-Wesley.

Bardi, A., Lacquiere, C., Fayol, M. and Lacert, P. (1998) 'Pathology of counting approach of a developmental dyscalculia.' *Annales de Readaptation et de Medecine Physique* **41**(8): 502–6.

Basic Skills Agency (1998). *Family Numeracy Adds Up*. London, NFER/BSA.

BEAM Education (2002). *Number Track Games*. London, BEAM Education.

BEAM Education (2003). *Starting Out: Foundation Stage Mathematics*. London, BEAM Education.

Bird, M. (1991). *Mathematics for Young Children: An Active Thinking Approach*. London, Routledge.

Blenkin, G. M. (1994). Early learning and a developmentally appropriate curriculum. In G. M. Blenkin and V. Kelly (eds) *The National Curriculum and Early Learning*. London, Paul Chapman Publishing.

Bliss, J., Askew, M. and Macrae, S. (1996). 'Effective teaching and learning: scaffolding revisited.' *Oxford Review of Education* **22**(1): 37–61.

Board of Education (1933). Infants and Nursery Schools: Report of the Consultative Committee of the Board of Education (Hadow). London, HMSO.

Bottle, G. (1999). 'A study of children's mathematical experiences in the home.' *Early Years* **20**(1): 53–64.

Boulton-Lewis, G. (1990). Young children's thinking strategies and levels of capacity. In L. P. Steffe and T. Wood (eds) *Transforming Children's Mathematics Education: International Perspectives*. Hillsdale, NJ, Lawrence Erlbaum Associates: 156–160.

Boulton-Lewis, G., Wilss, G. M. and Mutch, S. L. (1996). 'An analysis of young children's strategies and use of devices of length measurement.' *Journal of Mathematical Behaviour* 15: 329–347.

Brannon, E. M. and Van de Walle, G. A. (2001). 'The development of ordinal number competence in young children.' *Cognitive Psychology* 43: 53–81.

Briggs, R. (1973). *Jim and the Beanstalk*. Harmondsworth, Picture Puffin.

Brizuela, B. M. (2004). *Mathematical Development in Young Children: Exploring Notations*. New York, Teachers College Press.

Broadhead, P. (2004). *Early Years Play and Learning: Developing Social Skills and Cooperation*. London, RoutledgeFalmer.

Brown, A. L. and Palinscar, A. S. (1989). Guided, cooperative learning and individual knowledge acquisition. In L. R. Resnick (ed.) *Knowledge, Learning and Instruction*. Hillsdale, NJ, Lawrence Erlbaum Associates: 393–445.

Bruce, B. and Threlfall, J. (2004). 'One, two, three and counting.' *Educational Studies in Mathematics* 55: 3–26.

Bruce, T. (1991). *Time to Play*. London, Hodder & Stoughton.

Bruce, T. and L. Bartholomew (1993). *Getting to Know You*. London, Hodder & Stoughton.

Bruce, T. and Meggitt, C. (1996). *Childcare and Education*. London, Hodder & Stoughton.

Bruner, J. (1966). *Towards a Theory of Instruction*. Cambridge, MA, Harvard University Press.

Bruner, J. (1980). *Under 5 in Britain: The Oxford Pre-school Research Project*. London, Grant McIntyre.

Burton, L. (1984). *Thinking Things Through: Problem Solving in Mathematics*. London, Basil Blackwell.

Buxton, L. (1981). *Do you Panic about Maths? Coping with Maths Anxiety*. London, Heinemann Educational.

Carle, E. (1974). *The Very Hungry Caterpillar*. Harmondsworth, Picture Puffin.

Carpenter, T. P. and Moser, J. M. (1984). 'The acquisition of addition and subtraction concepts in grades one through three.' *Journal for Research in Mathematics Education* 15: 179–202.

Carr, M. (1992). Maths for meaning: tracing a path for early mathematics development. *SAME Papers 1992*. Hamilton, New Zealand, University of Waikato Centre for Science and Mathematics Research and Longman Paul.

Carr, M. (2001). *Assessment in Early Childhood Settings: Learning Stories*. London, Paul Chapman.

Carr, M., Peters, S. and Young-Loveridge, J. (1994). Early childhood mathematics: finding the right level of challenge. In J. Neyland (ed.) *Mathematics Education: A Handbook for Teachers, volume 1*. Wellington, New Zealand, Wellington College of Education. 271–282.

Carr, M., Young-Loveridge, J. and Peters, S. (1991). *The Informal Mathematics of Four Year Olds; Understanding its Purpose*. Fifth Early Childhood Convention, Dunedin, New Zealand.

Carraher, T. N., Carraher, D. W. and Schliemann, A. D. (1985). 'Mathematics in the streets and in schools.' *British Journal of Developmental Psychology* 3: 21–29.

Child, L. (2001). *I Am Not Sleepy and I Will Not Go to Bed*. London, Orchard.

Chukowsky, K. (1963). *From Two to Five*. Berkeley, University of California Press.

Clements, D. H. (1984). 'Training effects on the development and generalisation of Piagetian logical operations and knowledge of number.' *Journal of Educational Psychology* 76(5): 766–776.

Clements, D. H. (2004). Geometric and spatial thinking in early childhood education. In D. H. Clements and J. Sarama (eds) *Engaging Young Children in Mathematics: Standards for Early Childhood Mathematics Education*. Mahwah NJ, Lawrence Erlbaum Associates: 267–297.

Clements, D. H. and Stephan, M. (2004). Measurement in Pre-K to Grade 2 Mathematics. In D. H. Clements and J. Sarama (eds) *Engaging Young Children in Mathematics: Standards for Early Childhood Mathematics Education*. Mahwah, NJ, Lawrence Earlbaum Associates: 299–317.

Clements, D. H., Swaminathan, S., Zeitler, H. M. A. and Sarama, J. (1999). 'Young children's concepts of shape' *Journal for Research in Mathematics Education* 30(2): 192–212.

Cobb, P. and Whitenack, J. W. (1996). 'A method for conducting longitudinal analyses of classroom videorecordings and transcripts.' *Educational Studies in Mathematics* 30: 213–228.

Cohen, D. (1987). *The Development of Play*. London, Croom Helm.

Coltman, P., Petyaeva, D. and Anghileri, J. (2002). 'Scaffolding learning through meaningful tasks and adult interaction.' *Early Years* 22(1): 39–49.

Cook, D. (1996). 'Mathematical sense-making and role-play in the nursery.' *Early Child Development and Care* 121: 55–66.

Cooper, B. and Dunne, M. (2004). Constructing the 'legitimate' goal of a 'realistic' maths item: a comparison of 10–11 and 13–14 year olds. In B. Allen and S. Johnston-Wilder (eds) *Mathematics Education: Exploring the Culture of Learning*. London, Routledge: 69–90.

Cowan, R. (2003). Does it all add up? Changes in children's knowledge of addition combinations, strategies and principles. In A. J. Baroody and A. Dowker (eds) *The Development of Arithmetic Concepts and Skills.* Mahwah, NJ, Lawrence Earlbaum Associates: 35–74.

Cowan, R. and Foster, C. M. (1993). 'Encouraging children to count.' *British Journal of Developmental Psychology* **11**: 411–420.

Curtis, A. (1998). *A Curriculum for the Pre-school Child: Learning to Learn.* London, Routledge.

Dahlberg, G., Moss, P. and Pence, A. (1999). *Beyond Quality in Early Childhood Education and Care.* London, Falmer.

David, T. (1998) 'Learning properly? Young children and Desirable Outcomes.' *Early Years* **18**(2): 61–5.

Davis, G. and Pepper, K. (1992). 'Mathematical problem solving by preschool children.' *Educational Studies in Mathematics* **23**: 397–415.

Dehaene, S. (2001). 'Precis of the Number Sense.' *Mind and Language* **16**(1): 16–36.

Delgado, A. R. and Prieto, G. (2004). 'Cognitive mediators and sex-related differences in mathematics.' *Intelligence* **32**(1): 25–32.

Deloache, J. S. and Brown, A. L. (1987). The early emergence of planning skills in children. In J. Bruner and H. Haste (eds) *The Child's Construction of the World.* London, Methuen: 108–130.

Department of Education and Science (1990). *Starting with Quality: The Report of the Committee of Enquiry into the Quality of Educational Experience Offered to Three and Four Year Olds (the Rumbold Report).* London, HMSO.

DfEE/QCA (1999). *The National Curriculum: Handbook for Primary Teachers in England.* London, Qualifications and Curriculum Authority.

DfEE/QCA (2000). *Curriculum Guidance for the Foundation Stage.* London, QCA.

DfEE/QCA (2003). *Foundation Stage Profile Handbook.* London, QCA.

Dickson, L., Brown, M. and Gibson, O. (eds) (1984). *Children Learning Mathematics: A Teacher's Guide to Recent Research.* Eastbourne, Holt, Rinehart and Winston for the Schools Council.

Dijk, E. F., van Oers, B. and Terwel, J. (2004). 'Schematising in early childhood mathematics education: why, when and how?' *European Early Childhood Education Research Journal* **12**(1): 71–81.

Doig, B., McCrae, B. and Rowe, K. (2003). A Good Start to Numeracy: Effective numeracy strategies from research and practice in early childhood. www.acer.edu.au/goodstart/documents/GoodStart.pdf (accessed Feb 2005)

Donaldson, M. (1978). *Children's Minds*. London, Fontana.

Donlan, C. (2003). Early numeracy of children with Specific Learning Impairments. In A. J. Baroody (ed.) *The Development of Arithmetic Concepts and Skills*. Mahwah, NJ, Lawrence Earlbaum Asssociates: 337–358.

Dowling, M. (1992). *Education 3–5*. London, Paul Chapman.

Dufour-Janvier, B., Bednarz, N. and Belanger, M. (1987). Pedagogical considerations concerning the problem of representation. In C. Janvier (ed.) *Problems of Representation in the Teaching and Learning of Mathematics*. London, Lawrence Erlbaum Associates: 109–122.

Durkin, K., Shire, B., Riem, R., Crowther, R. D. and Rutter, D. R. (1986). 'The social and linguistic context of early number word use.' *British Journal of Developmental Psychology* **4**: 269–288.

Early Childhood Education Forum (1998). *Quality in Diversity in Early Learning: A Framework for Early Childhood Practice*. London, National Children's Bureau.

Early Childhood Mathematics Group (1997). *Learning Mathematics in the Nursery: Desirable Approaches*. London, BEAM.

Edgington, M. (1998). *The Nursery Teacher in Action*. London, Paul Chapman Publishing.

Edlin, W. and Hardy, D. (2002). *Video: Challenging Number at Triangle*. London, Triangle Nursery School, Lambeth. (Headteacher: Debbie Hardy.)

Elia, I. and Gagatsis, A. (2003). 'Young children's understanding of geometric shapes: the role of geometric models.' *European Early Childhood Education Research Journal* **11**(2): 43–61.

Evans, J. (2002). 'Talking about maths.' *Education 3–13* **30**(1 March): 66–71.

Eyken, V. d. (1977). *The Pre-school Years*. Harmondsworth, Penguin.

Fayol, M., Barrouillet, P. and Marinthe, C. (1998). 'Predicting arithmetical achievement from neuropsychological performance: a longitudinal study.' *Cognition* **68**: 863–870.

Fielker, D. (1973). 'A structural approach to primary school geometry.' *Mathematics Teaching* **63**: 12–17.

Fielker, D. (1976). 'Weight watching.' *Mathematics Teaching* **74**: 26–28.

Fielker, D. (1993). *Mental Geometry*. London, BEAM.

Fluck, M. and L. Henderson (1996). 'Counting and cardinality in English nursery pupils.' *British Journal of Educational Psychology* **66**: 501–517.

Foxman, D. (1994). The second international assessment of educational progress (IAEP2). *British Congress on Mathematical Education, University of Leeds July 1993: Research papers.* G. Wain. Leeds, University of Leeds.

Friedman, L. (1995). 'The space factor in mathematics: gender differences.' *Review of Educational Research* **65**(1): 22–50.

Fuson, K. (1988). *Children's Counting and Concepts of Number.* New York, Springer Verlag.

Fuson, K. and Hall, J. W. (1983). The acquisition of early number word meanings. In H. P. Ginsburg (ed.) *The Development of Mathematical Thinking.* New York, Academic Press: 49–107.

Fuson, K. C. and Kwon, Y. (1992). 'Korean children's single-digit addition and subtraction: numbers structured by ten.' *Journal for Research in Mathematics Education* **23**(2): 148–165.

Garvey, C. (1977). *Play.* London, Fontana.

Geary, D.C., Bow-Thomas, C.C. and Yao, Y. (1992). 'Counting knowledge and skill in cognitive addition: a comparison of normal and mathematically disabled children.' *Journal of Experimental Child Psychology* **54**: 372–91.

Gelman, R. and Gallistel, C. R. (1978). *The Child's Understanding of Number.* Cambridge, MA, Harvard University Press.

Gierl, M. J. and Bisanz, J. (1995). 'Anxieties and attitudes related to mathematics in grades 3 and 6.' *Journal of Experimental Education* **63**(2): 139–158.

Gifford, S. (1990). 'Young children's representations of number operations.' *Mathematics Teaching* **132**: 64–71.

Gifford, S. (1995). 'Number in early childhood.' *Early Child Development and Care* **109**: 95–115.

Gifford, S. (1997). When should they start doing sums? In I. Thompson (ed.) *Teaching and Learning Early Number.* Milton Keynes, Open University Press: 75–88.

Gifford, S. (2002). *Between the Secret Garden and the Hothouse: A Study of the Teaching and Learning of Number in a Nursery Setting.* London, Kings College London: 431.

Gifford, S., Barber, P. and Ebbutt, S. (1998). *Number in Nursery and Reception.* London, BEAM.

Ginsburg, H. P. (1977). *Children's Arithmetic: The Learning Process.* New York, NY, D. Van Nostrand.

Ginsburg, H. P. and Allardice, B. S. (1983). Children's psychological difficulties in mathematics. In H. P. Ginsburg (ed.) *The Development of Mathematical Thinking.* New York, Academic Press.

Ginsburg, H. P. and Baron, J. (1993). Cognition: young children's construction of mathematics. In R. R. Jensen (ed.) *Research Ideas for the Classroom: Early Childhood Mathematics*. New York, Macmillan: 3–21.

Ginsburg, H. P., Klein, A. and Starkey, P. (1998). The development of children's mathematical thinking: connecting research with practice. In I. E. Sigel and K. A. Renninger (eds) *Handbook of Child Psychology 4: Child Psychology in Practice*. NY, J. Wiley & Sons: 401–476.

Goodnow, J. (1977). *Children's Drawing*. Shepton Mallett, Fontana/Open Books.

Greenes, C., Ginsburg, H. P. and B. R. (2004). 'Big math for little kids.' *Early Childhood Research Quarterly* **19**(1): 159–166.

Griffin, S. (2004). 'Building number sense with number worlds: a mathematics program for young children.' *Early Childhood Research Quarterly* **19**: 173–180.

Griffiths, R. (1994). Mathematics and play. In J. Moyles (ed.) *The Excellence of Play*. Buckingham, Open University Press: 145–151.

Griffiths, R. (1995). *Young Children, Money and Shops*. Third British Congress of Mathematics Education, Manchester.

Griffiths, R. (2001). 'Money and shops, role-play and real life.' *Mathematics Teaching* (174).

Groen, G. T. and Resnick, L. B. (1977). 'Can pre-schoolers invent addition algorithms?' *Journal of Educational Psychology* **69**(6): 645–652.

Gura, P. (ed.) with the Froebel Blockplay Research Group directed by Tina Bruce (1992). *Exploring Learning: Young Children and Blockplay*. London, Paul Chapman Publishing Ltd.

Gussin Paley, V. (1981). *Wally's Stories*. Cambridge, MA, Harvard University Press.

Hargreaves, A. and Fullan, M. (1992). *Understanding Teacher Development*. London, Cassell.

Harries, T. (2000). *Mental Maths for the Numeracy Hour*. London, David Fulton.

Harrison, R. (1987). 'On fullness.' *Mathematics Teaching* (119): 27–28.

Heyman, G. D., Dweck, C. S. and Cain, K. M. (1992). 'Young children's vulnerability to self blame and helplessness: relationship to beliefs about goodness.' *Child Development* **63**(2): 401–415.

HM Chief Inspector of Schools (1993). *First Class: The Standards and Quality of Education in Reception Classes*. London, HMSO.

HM Inspectors of Schools (1989). *Aspects of Primary Education: The Education of Children Under Five*. London, HMSO.

Hopkins, C., Pope, S. and Pepperell, S. (2004). *Understanding Primary Mathematics*. London, David Fulton Publishers.

Hughes, M. (1981). 'Can pre-school children add and subtract?' *Educational Psychology* **1**(3): 207–219.

Hughes, M. (1986). *Children and Number: Difficulties in Learning Mathematics*. Oxford, Basil Blackwell.

Hutchins, P. (1983). *You'll Soon Grow into Them, Titch*. London, Bodley Head.

Hutchins, P. (1986). *The Doorbell Rang*. London, Bodley Head.

Hutt, S. J., Tyler, S. and Christopherson, H. (1989). *Play, Exploration and Learning: A Natural History of the Pre-school*. London, Routledge.

Inkpen, M. (1993). *Kipper's Toy Box*. Sevenoaks, Hodder & Stoughton.

Inkpen, M. (1998). *The Great Pet Sale*. London, Hodder Children's Books.

Isaacs, E. B., Edmonds, C. J., Lucas, A. and Gadian, D. G. (2001). 'Calculation difficulties in children of very low birthweight.' *Brain* **124**: 1701–1707.

Isaacs, S. (1930). *Intellectual Growth in Young Children*. London, Routledge.

Jones, K. and Mooney, C. (2003). Making space for geometry in primary mathematics. I. Thompson (ed.) *Enhancing Primary Mathematics Teaching*. Maidenhead, Open University Press: 3–15.

Jones, L. (1998). 'Home and school numeracy for young Somali pupils in Britain.' *European Early Childhood Education Research Journal* **6**(1): 63–71.

Jordan, N. C., Hanich, L. B. and Uberti, H. Z. (2003). Mathematical thinking and learning difficulties. In A. J. Baroody and A. Dowker (eds) *The Development of Arithmetic Concepts and Skills*. Mahwah, NJ, Lawrence Earlbaum Associates: 359–383.

Jordan, N. C. and Montani, T. O. (1997). 'Cognitive arithmetic and problem solving: a comparison of children with specific and general mathematics learning difficulties.' *Journal of Learning Disabilities* **30**(6): 624–634, 684.

Kamii, C. (1985). *Young Children Reinvent Arithmetic: Implications of Piaget's Theory*. New York, Teacher's College.

Katz, L. G. (1995). *Talks with Teachers of Young Children*. Norwood, NJ, Ablex Publishing Corporation.

Kaufmann, L., Handl, P. and Thony, B. (2003). 'Evaluation of a numeracy intervention programme focusing on basic numerical knowledge and conceptual knowledge.' *Journal of Learning Disabilities* **36**(6): 564–573.

Kerslake, D. (1975). 'Taking Time Out.' *Mathematics Teaching* (73): 8–10.

Kleinberg, S. and Menmuir, J. (1995). 'Perceptions of mathematics in pre-five settings.' *Education 3 to 13* (October): 29–35.

Kobayashi, T., Hraki, T. and Hasegawa, T. (2004). 'Baby arithmetic: one object plus one tone.' *Cognition* **91**: B23–B34.

Laevers, F. (1993). 'Deep level learning: an exemplary application on the area of physical knowledge.' *European Early Childhood Education Research Journal* **1**(1): 53–68.

Laevers, F. (2000). 'Forward to basics! Deep level learning and the experiential approach.' *Early Years* **20**(2): 20–29.

Lave, J. (1988). *Cognition in Practice: Mind, Mathematics and Culture in Everyday Life*. Cambridge, Cambridge University Press.

Lee, G.-L. (1997). 'The characteristics of early childhood education in Korea.' *International Journal of Early Childhood* **29**(2): 44–50.

Lerman, S. (2000). The social turn in mathematics education research. In J. Boaler (ed.) *Multiple Perspectives on Mathematics Teaching and Learning*. Westport, CT & London, Ablex Publishing: 19–44.

Liben, L. S. and Yekel, C. A. (1996). 'Preschoolers' understanding of plan and oblique maps: the role of geometric and representational correspondence.' *Child Development* **67**(6): 2780–2796.

Lieberman, N. J. (1977). *Playfulness: Its Relationship to Imagination and Creativity*. New York, Academic Press.

Ma, X. and Kishor, N. (1997). 'Assessing the relationship between attitude toward mathematics and achievement in mathematics: a meta-analysis.' *Journal for Research in Mathematics Education* **28**(1): 26–47.

Mac Naughton, G. (2003). *Shaping Early Childhood*. Maidenhead, Open University Press.

Mannigel, D. (1988). 'Enhancing autonomy: implications for maths (and other) education and classroom organisation in early childhood.' *Australian Journal of Early Childhood* **13**(1): 3–7.

Marton, F. and Neuman, D. (1990). Constructivism, phenomenology and the origin of arithmetic skills. In C. P. Steffe and T. Wood (eds) *Transforming Children's Mathematics Education*. New Jersey, Lawrence Earlbaum Associates: 63–75.

McGarrigle, J. and Donaldson, M. (1974). 'Conservation accidents.' *Cognition* **3**: 341–350.

McLeod, D. B. (1992). Research on affect in mathematics education: a reconceptualisation. In D. A. Grouws (ed.) *Handbook of Research on Mathematics Teaching and Learning*. New York, NY, Macmillan: 575–596.

Meadows, S. and Cashdan, A. (1988). *Helping Children Learn*. London, Fulton.

Mix, K. S., Huttenlocher, J. and Levine, S. C. (2002). *Quantitative Development in Infancy and Early Childhood*. Oxford, Oxford University Press.

Moyles, J., Adams, S. and Musgrove, A. (2002). *Study of Pedagogical*

Effectiveness in Early Learning (SPEEL), Research Report 363. London, DfES.

Munn, P. (1994). 'The early development of literacy and numeracy skills.' *European Early Childhood Education Research Journal* 2(1): 5–18.

Munn, P. (1996). Teaching and learning in the pre-school period. In M. Hughes (ed.) *Teaching and Learning in Changing Times*. Oxford, Blackwell: 109–128.

Munn, P. (1997). Children's beliefs about counting. In I. Thompson (ed.) *Teaching and Learning Early Number*. Buckingham, Open University Press: 9–19.

Munn, P. and Schaffer, H. R. (1993). 'Literacy and numeracy events in socially interactive contexts.' *International Journal of Early Years Education* 1(3): 61–80.

National Association for the Education of Young Children (2002). *Early Childhood Mathematics: Promoting Good Beginnings*. Statement of the National Association for the Education of Young Children (NAEYC) and the National Council of Teachers of Mathematics (NCTM). Washington, DC.

National Numeracy Strategy (2002). *Mathematical Activities for the Foundation Stage*. London, Department for Education and Skills.

New Zealand Ministry of Education (1993). *Te Whariki: Draft Guidelines for Developmentally Appropriate Programmes in Early Childhood Services*. Wellington, NZ Ministry of Education/Learning Media.

Nunes, T. and Bryant, P. (1996). *Children Doing Mathematics*. Oxford, Blackwell.

Nutbrown, C. (1999). *Threads of Thinking*. London, Sage.

Ontario Ministry of Education (2003). *Early Math Strategy: The Report of the Expert Panel on Early Math in Ontario*.

Pascal, C. and Bertram, T. (1997). *Effective Early Learning: Case Studies in Improvement*. London, Hodder and Stoughton.

Payne, J. N. and Huinker, D. M. (1993). Early number and numeration. In R. R. Jensen (ed.) *Research Ideas for the Classroom: Early Childhood Mathematics*. New York, Macmillan: 43–70.

Pengelly, H. (1985). *Mathematics: Making Sure*. Perth, University of Western Australia.

Peters, S. (1998). 'Playing games and learning mathematics: the results of two intervention studies.' *International Journal of Early Years Education* 6: 49–58.

Piaget, J. (1947). *The Psychology of Intelligence*. London, Routledge & Kegan Paul.

Piaget, J. (1951). *Play, Dreams and Imitation in Childhood*. London, Routledge & Kegan Paul.

Piaget, J. (1952). *The Child's Conception of Number*.

Piaget, J. (1969). *The Child's Conception of Time*. London, Routledge & Kegan Paul.

Piaget, J. (1973). *Comments on Mathematical Education*. Developments in Mathematical Education, Proceedings of the Second International Congress on Mathematical Education, Exeter, Cambridge University Press.

Piaget, J. and Inhelder, B. (1956). *The Child's Conception of Space*. London, Routledge & Kegan Paul.

Piaget, J., Inhelder, B. and Szeminska, A. (1960). *The Child's Conception of Geometry*. London, Routledge and Kegan Paul.

Pollard, A. and Filer, A. (1996). *The Social World of Children's Learning: Case Studies of Pupils from Four to Seven*. London, Cassell.

Pound, L., Cook, L., Court, J., Stevenson, J. and Wadsworth, J. (1992). *The Early Years: Mathematics*. London, Harcourt Brace Javonovich.

Reggio Children (1997). *Shoe and Metre: Children and Measurement*. Reggio Emilia, Reggio Children Srl.

Resnick, L.B. (1983). A developmental theory of number understanding. In H. Ginsburg (ed.) The development of mathematical thinking. New York, Academic Press.

Rhydderch-Evans, Z. (2002). 'Attitude is everything.' *Mathematics Teaching* 181: 20–23.

Roberts, R. (1995). *Self-esteem and Successful Early Learning*. London, Hodder & Stoughton.

Robson, B. (1983). 'Encouraging dialogue in pre-school units: the role of the pink pamfer.' *Educational Review* 35(2): 141–148.

Rogers, J. (1997). 'Shopping around for answers.' *Times Educational Supplement* (11 July): 12.

Rogers, J. E. (1996). 'Children as apprentices to number.' *Early Child Development and Care* 125: 15–25.

Rogoff, B. (1990). *Apprenticeship in Thinking: Cognitive Development in Social Context*. New York, Oxford University Press.

Rogoff, B. (1990). The joint socialisation of development by young children and adults. In V. Lee (ed.) *Children's Learning in School*. London, Hodder & Stoughton in association with The Open University: 41–58.

Rosen, M. (2001). *We're Going on a Bear Hunt*. London, Walker.

Rubin, Z. (1980). *Children's Friendships*. London, Fontana.

Sammons, P., Sylva, K., Melhuish, E., Siraj-Blatchford, I., Taggart, B. and

Elliot, K. (2002). *Measuring the Impact of Pre-school on Children's Cognitive Progress over the Pre-school Period*, Technical Paper 8a. London, Institute of Education, University of London.

Sarama, J. (2004). Technology in early childhood mathematics: building blocks as an innovative technology-based curriculum. In D. H. Clements, J. Sarama and A. M. DiBiase (eds) *Engaging Young Children in Mathematics: Standards for Early Childhood Mathematics Education*. Mahwah, NJ, Lawrence Erlbaum Associates: 361–375.

Sarama, J. and Clements, D. H. (2004). 'Building blocks for early childhood mathematics.' *Early Childhood Research Quarterly* 19: 181–189.

Saxe, G. B., Becker, J., Sadeghpour, M., and Sicilian, S. (1989). 'Development differences in children's understanding of number word conventions.' *Journal for Research in Mathematics Education* 20(5): 468–488.

Saxe, G., Guberman, S. and Gearhart, M. (1987). 'Social processes in early number development.' *SRCD Monograph, Serial no. 216* 52(2).

Schaeffer, B., Eggleston, V. H. and Scott, J. L. (1974). 'Number development in young children.' *Cognitive Psychology* 6: 357–379.

School Curriculum and Assessment Authority (1996). *Nursery Education: Desirable Outcomes for Children's Learning*. London, DfEE/SCAA.

Schools Council (1978). *Early Mathematical Experiences*. London, Addison Wesley.

Siraj-Blatchford, I., Sylva, K., Muttock, S., Gilden, R. and Bell, D. (2002). *Researching Effective Pedagogy in the Early Years* (REPEY), Research Report 356. London, Department for Education and Skills.

Smith, A. (1998). *Accelerated Learning in Practice*. Trowbridge, Redwood Books.

Sophian, C. (2004). 'Mathematics for the future: developing a Head Start curriculum to support mathematics learning.' *Early Childhood Research Quarterly* 19(1): 59–81.

Starkey, P., Klein, A. Wakeley, A. (2004). 'Enhancing young children's mathematical knowledge through a pre-kindergarten mathematics intervention.' *Early Childhood Research Quarterly* 19: 99–120.

Steffe L, Firth, D. et al. (1981). 'On the nature of counting activity: perceptual unit items.' *For the Learning of Mathematics* 2(July): 13–21.

Steffe, L., von Glaserfeld, E., Richards, J. and Cobb, P. (1983). *Children's Counting Types: Philosophy Theory and Application*. New York, Praeger.

Stephen, C. and Wilkinson, J. E. (1999). 'Rhetoric and reality in developing language and mathematical skills: plans and playroom experiences.' *Early Years* 19(2): 62–73.

Stevenson, H., Lee, S.-Y., Chen, C. and Lummis, M. (1990). 'Mathematical achievement of children in China and the United States.' *Child Development* **61**: 1063–1066.

Stoessinger, R. and Edmunds, J. (1990). 'Using natural learning processes in mathematics.' *Mathematics in School* (May): 30–33.

Sugarman, I. (1997). Teaching for strategies. In I. Thompson (ed.) *Teaching and Learning Early Number*. Buckingham, Open University Press: 142–154.

Swan, M. (2003). Making sense of mathematics. In I. Thompson (ed.) *Enhancing Primary Mathematics Teaching*. Maidenhead, Open University Press: 112–124.

Sylva, K. (1984). 'A hard headed look at the fruits of play.' *Early Child Development and Care* **15**: 171–184.

Sylva, K., Roy, C. and Painter, M. (1980). *Childwatching at Playgroup and Nursery School: Oxford Preschool Research Project*. London, Grant McIntyre.

Sylva, K. and Wiltshire, J. (1993). 'The impact of early learning on children's later development: a review prepared for the RSA inquiry "Start Right".' *European Early Childhood Education Research Journal* **1**(1): 17–40.

Tharp, R. and Gallimore, R. (1988). *Rousing Minds to Life: Teaching, Learning and Schooling in Social Context*. Cambridge, Cambridge University Press.

Thatcher, F. (1998). *Ten Little Elephants*. Kettering, Oyster Books.

The Royal Society, J. M. C. (2001). *Teaching and Learning Geometry 11–19*. London, The Royal Society.

Thomas, G. and Tagg, A. (2003). Exploring Issues in Mathematics Education: An Evaluation of the Early Numeracy Project 2003, New Zealand Ministry of Education.

Thompson, I. (2000). 'Teaching place value in the UK: time for a reappraisal?' *Educational Review* **52**(3): 291–298.

Thorpe, P. (1995). 'Spatial concepts and young children.' *International Journal of Early Years Education* **3**(2): 63–73.

Thumpston, G. (1994). Mathematics in the National Curriculum: implications for learning in the early years. In G. M. Blenkin and A. V. Kelly (eds) *The National Curriculum and Early Learning*. London, Paul Chapman.

Tizard, B., Blatchford, P., Burke, J., Farquhar, C. and Plewis, I. (1988). *Young Children at School in the Inner City*. New York, Lawrence Erlbaum Associates.

Tizard, B. and Hughes, M. (1984). *Young Children Learning*. London, Fontana.

Tobin, J. J., Wu, D. Y. H. and Davidson, D. H. (1989). *Preschool in Three Cultures*. New Haven.

Tudge, J. R. H. (1992). 'Processes and consequences of peer collaboration: a Vygotskian analysis.' *Child Development* **63**: 1364–1379.

Van de Rijt, B. and Van Luit, J. E. H. (1998). 'Effectiveness of the Additional Early Mathematics program for teaching children early mathematics.' *Instructional Science* **26**: 337–358.

van Hiele, P. M. (1986). *Structure and Insight*. Orlando, FL, Academic Press.

Vygotsky, L. S. (1978). *Mind in Society*. Cambridge, MA, Harvard University Press.

Vygotsky, L. S. (1986). *Thought and Language*. Cambridge, MA, MIT Press.

Walkerdine, V. (1988). *The Mastery of Reason: Cognitive Development and the Production of Rationality*. London, Routledge.

Walkerdine, V. (1989). *Counting Girls Out*. London, Virago.

Whitehead, M. (1995). Nonsense, rhyme and wordplay in young children. In R. Beard (ed.) *Rhyme, Reading and Writing*. London, Hodder & Stoughton: 42–61.

Wing, T. (2001). 'Serendipity, and a special need.' *Mathematics Teaching* (174): 27–30.

Womack, D. (1993). 'Game, set and match.' *Times Educational Supplement* (8 October): XX–XXI.

Wood, D. (1988). *How Children Think and Learn*. Oxford, Basil Blackwell.

Wood, D. (1991). Aspects of teaching and learning. In P. Light, S. Sheldon and M. Woodhead (eds) *Learning to Think*. London, Routledge.

Wood, D. J., Bruner, J. S. and Ross, G. (1976). 'The role of tutoring in problem solving.' *Journal of Child Psychology and Psychiatry* **17**: 89–100.

Worthington, M. and Carruthers, E. (2003). *Children's Mathematics: Making Marks, Making Meaning*. London, Paul Chapman Publishing.

Wright, R. J. (1994). 'A study of the numerical development of 5-year-olds and 6-year-olds.' *Educational Studies in Mathematics* **26**: 25–44.

Wright, R. J., Martland, J. and Stafford, A. K. (2000). *Early Numeracy: Assessment for Teaching and Intervention*. London, Chapman.

Wynn, K. (1990). 'Children's understanding of counting.' *Cognition* **36**: 155–193.

Xu, F. (2003). 'Numerosity discrimination in infants: evidence of two systems of representation.' *Cognition* **89**: B15–25.

Yeo, D. (2003). *Dyslexia, Dyspraxia and Mathematics*. London, Whurr.

Young, J. (1994). *Young Children's Apprenticeship in Number*. Unpublished PhD, University of London.

Young-Loveridge, J. (1989). 'The relationship between children's home experiences and their mathematical skills on entry to school.' *Early child Development and Care* **43**: 43–59.

Young-Loveridge, J. (1991). *The Development of Children's Number Concepts from ages five to nine*. Hamilton, New Zealand, University of Waikato.

Young-Loveridge, J. (1993). *The Effects of Early Mathematics Intervention: The EMI-5s Study*. Hamilton, New Zealand, University of Waikato.

Young-Loveridge, J. (2002). 'Early childhood numeracy: building an understanding of part-whole relationships.' *Australian Journal of Early Childhood* **27**(4): 36–40.

Young-Loveridge, J. (2004). 'Effects on early numeracy of a program using number books and games.' *Early Childhood Research Quarterly* **19**(1): 82–98.

Young-Loveridge, J., Carr, M. and Peters, S. (1995). *Enhancing the Mathematics of Four Year-olds: The EMI-4s Study*. Hamilton, New Zealand, School of Education, University of Waikato.

Zacharos, K. and Ravanis, K. (2000). 'The transformation of natural to geometrical concepts, concerning children 5–7 years old. The case of measuring surfaces.' *European Early Childhood Education Research Journal* **8**(2): 63–72.

Zur, O. and Gelman, R. (2004). 'Young children can add and subtract by predicting and checking.' *Early Childhood Research Quarterly* **19**(1): 121–137.

Index

Page numbers in italics indicate illustrations; those in bold indicate major references.

Related books from Open University Press

Purchase from www.openup.co.uk or order through your local bookseller

MAKING SENSE OF CHILDREN'S DRAWINGS

Angela Anning and Kathy Ring

If you know and love young children, find a way to read this book. Here you will discover the hidden talents of young children for complexity, design, and tenacity for learning . . . This book is a wonderful addition to the too-small library of quality books on young children's learning through art.

> Shirley Brice Heath, Professor Emerita, Stanford University and Professor at Large, Brown University USA

This book is unique in giving an in-depth account of the way young children approach drawing at home and at school. It shows the cognitive value of drawing in children's intellectual and emotional development and sets out the truly extraordinary range of drawing types that are used and understood by three to six year olds . . . It is an invaluable experience.

> Professor Ken Baynes, Department of Design and Technology, Loughborough University

This book explores how young children learn to draw and draw to learn, both at home and at school. It provides support for practitioners in developing a pedagogy of drawing in Art and Design and across the curriculum, and provides advice for parents about how to make sense of their children's drawings.

Making Sense of Children's Drawings is enlivened with the real drawings of seven young children collected over three years. These drawings stimulated dialogues with the children, parents and practitioners whose voices are reported in the book. The book makes a powerful argument for us to rethink radically the role of drawing in young children's construction of meaning, communication and sense of identity. It provides insights into the influence of media and consumerism, as reflected in popular visual imagery, and on gender identity formation in young children. It also offers strong messages about the overemphasis on the three Rs in early childhood education.

Key reading for students, practitioners and parents who want to encourage young children's drawing development without 'interfering' with their creativity, and who need a novel approach to tuning into young children's passions and preoccupations.

Contents

152pp   0 335 21265 4 (Paperback)   0 335 21266 2 (Hardback)

EARLY EXPLORATIONS IN SCIENCE
SECOND EDITION
Jane Johnston

Reviewers' comments on the first edition:

> Jane Johnston communicates a sense of effervescent enthusiasm for teaching and science, and her treatment is comprehensive.
>
> *TES*

> At last! A serious attempt to explore the scientific potential of infant and pre-school children . . . The author explains how scientific skills can be developed at an early stage, stimulating the natural inquisitive streak in children. This book . . . will start you thinking about science in a much more positive light.
>
> *Child Education*

This accessible and practical book supports good scientific practice in the early years. It helps practitioners to be creative providers, and shows them how to develop awe and wonder of the world in the children they teach. The book highlights the importance of a motivating learning environment and skilled interaction with well-trained adults. In addition, fundamental issues are explored such as the range, nature and philosophical under-pinning of early years experiences and the development of emergent scientific skills, understandings and attitudes.

New features for this edition include:

- An extended age range encompassing early learning from 0 – 8
- Updated material for the Foundation Stage Curriculum for 3 – 5-year-olds and the National Curriculum 2000 for 5 – 8-year-olds
- A new chapter focusing on conceptual understanding and thinking skills in the early years
- An emphasis on the importance of informal learning and play in early development

The book introduces and discusses new research and thinking in early years and science education throughout, making it relevant for current practice. This is an indispensable resource for all trainee and practising primary school teachers and early years practitioners.

c.208pp   0 335 21472 X (Paperback)